GETTING THERE

A SIMPLE GUIDE TO REACHING YOUR DREAMS BY SETTING GOALS

CARLETON "HOLLY" HOLLISTER

ARPress
ILLUMINATING IDEAS.
EMPOWERING VOICES

ARPress LLC
45 Dan Road Suite 5
Canton MA 02021
Hotline: 1(888) 821-0229
Fax: 1(508) 545-7580

Ordering Information:
Quantity sales. Special discounts are available on quantity purchases by corporations, associations, and others. For details, contact the publisher at the address above.

Printed in the United States of America.

ISBN-13:   Softcover   979-8-89330-452-7
              eBook   979-8-89330-453-4

Library of Congress Control Number: 2024900771

To those in my life who took the time to mentor and encourage me to be better. My wife and kids are the best of this list. I love you, Shelley, Jackson, and Ericca.

CONTENTS

THIS IS THE YEAR

Author Unknown

This is the year for making changes
This is the year for moving on
This is the year of overcoming
This is the year for growing strong.

This is the year for a new way of thinking
This is the year for making plans
This is the year for reaching out and
This is the year for joining hands.

This is the year that I put into action
All my desires and all of my means
This is the year that I follow my passion
This is the year to follow my dreams

I cannot change the ones that I love
This is the year I turn it over
This is the year I rise above
This is my time as an overcomer.

This is the year that I take my intention
Turn away from distraction and talk
This is the year I take a step and
This is the year I walk the walk.

This is the year I follow through
This is the year I move ahead
On all of the things I want to do
All the ideas that are in my head.

Gone are the lonely nights of yearning
Gone are the dark and cloudy skies
All the unsteady bridges burning
All of the doubt and all of the lies.

This is the chance to renew my commitment
To myself and those that I love
This is the moment for living fully
This is the time I rise above.

This is the chance to recapture power
This is the time to abandon fear
This is the moment, the finest hour
This is the year.
This is the year!

Make it your year!

MY STORY: FINDING MY OWN WAY TO FINANCIAL CONFIDENCE

As many people approach retirement, they regret that they didn't pursue specific dreams and goals more intentionally. Regret is a terrible feeling.

Before we discuss specific strategies for avoiding regret in life, I want to share with you a glimpse of my growing-up years. The story I am about to tell you relates directly to the reason I am a financial advisor, and it demonstrates how many of us, without a real plan or goal in place, can wander aimlessly and waste many good years. This is my own story about how *getting there*—to your ideal future—takes years of conscious planning and of overcoming a lifetime of aimlessness.

> *Getting there* takes years of conscious planning and of overcoming a lifetime of aimlessness.

I grew up in the Midwest in a great family. My dad was a professor at Bowling Green State University (BGSU), while my mom stayed at home and took care of four kids; I am the oldest of the four. We were a busy, churchgoing family, and my dad made sure we did things together. Sometimes my grandparents were involved, and sometimes it was just the six of us.

One of the most important things we did was vacation together every year. From the time I was nine, we went to Loughborough Lake, near Kingston, Ontario, Canada. We started out staying for ten days each time, and by the time I was in high school, we spent the entire summer there. With Dad's academic schedule, he had the summers off. We had friends at home and friends at the lake. We spent our days swimming, water skiing, and picnicking on the island. They are some of the best memories we have as a family.

My Dad's Money Struggles

I adored my father, but he had some issues. For most of my life, he weighed about 325 pounds. He would diet occasionally but was never very successful at managing it. Because Dad did not control his weight, there was never any direction or restriction on what the kids ate. Thus, three of us kids have struggled with our weight most of our lives.

Also, Dad was a chronic procrastinator. He was the guy who was at the library on April 14th, getting his tax forms that needed to be completed by midnight the following day. I never remember any real direction or discussion about setting and achieving personal goals.

As a professor at a State of Ohio university, he was covered by the state pension system. At the time, a retiring professor with thirty years of service could retire with about 80 percent of his regular full-time pay. Because of this pension, Dad never saved or set any funds aside for his retirement. He never had to save for our college, either, because we were allowed to go to BGSU tuition-free. Room and board costs were our responsibility, or we could commute from home.

I don't remember any conversations or instruction about saving money, life insurance protection, or general financial concepts. At the time, it didn't seem like a big deal. That generation was quite secretive about their personal finances, and Dad felt it was the man's responsibility to handle the money for the family. He never shared any of those things with Mom or anybody else, that I am aware of. He never had a financial advisor or person whom he relied on for financial direction and advice.

My dad had many, many fine qualities that I have benefitted from greatly. He loved his wife and family deeply, had lofty goals and ideals that he pursued with passion, achieved full professorship in mathematics, and served his church and community with his time and talent in many different capacities.

Unfortunately, he also had shortcomings that deeply affected me and other members of my family.

A few years after I graduated from high school, I moved away from home. I had known that Dad had some short-term money troubles, but they never seemed like a big deal. He seemed to manage those situations quietly, never wanting my mother to know. Apparently, this had been going on for some time—and it was about to come to a head.

One day, my mom ran into a friend of hers in the grocery store. She was the wife of a couple who were friends of my parents. The lady told Mom that Dad had borrowed money from her husband and that he was overdue in paying it back. You can imagine Mom's embarrassment. Later that night, she confronted Dad about the situation. I cannot imagine how hard that was for Mom, but it allowed the painful truth to be exposed. My dad had made a series of very bad financial decisions and had not shared them with her or others who could assist him.

Over the next several weeks, the truth began to come out about how much money my dad owed and to whom. Because he had never shared any of the problems with my mother, she felt betrayed. He also had not shared the problem with me or my siblings in an appropriate and honest way. One of the most devastating effects was that my folks had to move out of their house to a different place, and my mom was totally embarrassed. It put enormous pressure on their marriage, and I later found out they had considered separating.

Over time, they managed to bring the debt under control and keep the marriage together. Dad realized he needed some help and reached out to a colleague for some guidance. I cannot describe to you the pain, anguish, and distrust this situation created in our "perfect" Midwest churchgoing family.

It took a great deal of time for the entire family to begin to trust again. Even as I write this thirty years later, I feel a great deal of emotion about it.

This situation had a dramatic effect on my siblings and me, impacting financial decisions about our families. This painful experience led me to make financial planning my life's work. I started by getting my own financial house in order. Then I began helping others get out of debt. Finally, I made financial advising my career. I wanted to make sure that neither my family nor any other family ever experienced that same pain.

Each of us adult children has determined to be chain breakers, making our personal finances a priority. A key ingredient of this objective is sharing financial information with our spouses to ensure that the family is all on the same page.

I Realized I Was Following My Dad's Patterns

My ability to get my own financial house in order, and to help others do the same, took some time to happen, though.

I did not realize I had picked up several of my father's undesirable traits. I remember procrastinating on some tasks in college and struggling to meet deadlines. Once I joined the workforce, procrastination began causing me issues on the job. I would put things off until the last minute or make excuses for not getting things done.

In my early work years, I received many corrections from my supervisors that were a result of procrastination. One day my boss said to me, "You know the schedule is due every Friday. If you turn it in late one more time, we will be having a serious discussion about your future here." Suddenly, I was face-to-face with a fault that I had picked up from my father. Also, I was overweight and did not attempt to control my weight. I was sadly out of shape and was only twenty-four at the time.

For about six years, I worked as a restaurant manager. Not being married, I loved the work and didn't mind the long hours. Most everybody was single, so there was a camaraderie and a party environment. Over time, it became quite clear that this was not the business to be in if you wanted to be a family man.

But I worked when everyone else played—nights, weekends, and holidays. The pay was not high, especially for the number of hours required. Many of my colleagues struggled with alcohol, and those who were married struggled with the hours and demands of the job. It was a valuable learning ground, but it was not where I wanted to be long-term.

Over those six years, I lost weight and gained it back, never mastering the art of keeping it off. I was a hard worker but had a few traits that weren't the most desired. Besides the procrastination, we Hollisters all think we know a better way. If my supervisor was strong, then I was fine. However, if my manager was weak or was not confident in his job, then I was ready to lead—and that is not well-received. I found that the hard work was not enough. I was going to need to learn other traits if I was going to be a good employee, regardless of where I worked.

A Mentor Steps in at a Critical Time in My Career

In 1984, I moved to Erie, Pennsylvania. I had family there, and I took a sales job with a company based in my hometown of Bowling Green. I had a sales territory that covered the area between

Cleveland, Pittsburgh, and Buffalo. There were many small towns in the area. Back then, each small town had a retail center. I cold-called retailers in their shops, selling a variety of packaging items: price markers, printed bags, labels, and tags printed with the client's logo. It was a way for small retailers to get their name in front of customers.

As usual, I jumped in with both feet. It was hard establishing a territory, but slowly and surely, I progressed. In 1988, I was one of one hundred reps across the United States and was smack-dab in the middle of the pack. I wasn't doing poorly, but I was not doing nearly as well as I or my company would have liked me to do. One day, they sent the regional sales manager out to work with me. I was not thrilled. In my mind, I was doing fine.

What could this manager possibly teach me that I didn't already know?

Well, to shorten a long story, he worked with me for the day. He was complimentary of some of the things I did and made suggestions when needed. He did not criticize, so I took it pretty well. That afternoon, we made a call on a retailer. The call was not going well, and apparently, I began to argue with the client—softly, but still arguing.

After that call, the manager and I found a place to have a soft drink. He began to teach me about the sales process. He taught me to ask questions to help determine what a client's needs were—instead of telling the prospect how excellent our product was.

He also asked me what my goals were each day. I glibly responded that my goal was to write as much business as possible. "What a stupid question," I thought. He also gave me some challenges to begin working on, and he helped me set some goals for the coming work weeks. How many calls would I make, and how many sales did I expect to get?

I had no idea the impact that would have on me.

As I began working on my sales skills, I also pressed myself to make more calls. I discovered that when I asked clients questions instead of talking at them, they began to respond favorably. The more favorably they responded, the more calls I wanted to make.

> I discovered that when I asked clients questions instead of talking at them, they began to respond favorably.

The manager came back and worked with me a couple of weeks later. Over the remaining six months, we had a weekly phone conversation, mainly about my sales numbers, thereby allowing me to ask him questions about the sales process. He also suggested a couple of Zig Ziglar sales books. At first, I thought they were corny, but the process began to improve, and so did my sales.

In January of every year, the company would have a national sales conference, and every sales rep would come from across the United States to attend. It was an excellent opportunity to meet others doing the same thing and to learn from each other.

A key event at the conference was the banquet on the last evening. They always announced the top ten salespeople in the company. Although I did not qualify, I received an award for the most improved salesperson. As a result of the training and effort, I had gone from being ranked number 50 to number 12, out of 100 salespeople. I was thrilled, and during my brief acceptance speech, I gave credit to the sales manager for his effort and guidance.

From then on, I was ranked in the top ten for the rest of my career. A friend and I would battle for the fifth and sixth positions each year. It seemed that the top four were not going anywhere, but the two of us still qualified. Over time, this gave me many opportunities with the company, including working trade shows and eventually becoming a regional trainer and sales manager.

The manager really helped me. If I had blown him off and ignored his direction, I am confident that I would not have gotten the results I did. At some point, I would have probably left the company on my own or by invitation. The guidance and direction were essential, but they were not nearly as crucial as my attitude and willingness to embrace the training and learn goal setting on my own.

"As iron sharpens iron, so one person
sharpens another."
—Proverbs 27:17

I Became an Avid Goal Setter

Since 1988, I have been an avid goal setter. I have an entire notebook for my goals—one-year, three-year, and five-year goals. Some are just listed to accomplish at any time. One of those goals has been writing and publishing this book. I started it at least twenty years ago. However, raising kids and starting my own business left me little time to work on it. Besides, I needed twenty more years of training and examples so I could share them with you!

Goal setting has saved me from many problems or issues. Because of the drama and pain that came to my family as a result of my father's financial problems, it became a real focus in my life so I could make sure the same thing didn't happen to me. Being single until I was thirty-three, I had set some savings goals and began to learn about investing. When my wife and I got married in 1989, we both had savings and were able to purchase a home instead of having to rent the obligatory "first apartment."

I continued to read and learn about proper financial strategies and habits. In 1990, my wife and I put a plan together to eliminate our credit-card debt, and then we focused on paying the house off as soon as possible. We were both working and had no kids, so we could put extra dollars toward the mortgage. We managed to pay off the credit cards, but then I got very sick. Over the next several months, I had several doctors' visits and tests. They had me on a variety of medications that made it hard to function at times.

At the time, I was still a straight-commission salesperson, driving as much as two hours in one direction each day to service my territory. It became hard for me to drive throughout my sales territory, which resulted in lost income. Also, a large number of medical bills began to mount. Yes, we had insurance, but if you have been down this road, you know how quickly the bills can add up. Those bills, combined with my decreasing income, put a great deal of pressure on our finances.

Because we had eliminated all debt other than our mortgage, we were able to weather the storm. We set up payment plans for some of the medical bills and paid them over several months. We paid only the personal bills that had to be paid and the minimum on our mortgage. It took almost two years to dig out from under the mountain of medical bills.

I often think that we might not have survived financially if we hadn't made those important decisions before the crisis came.

Over the years, I have set goals in almost every aspect of my life. As my wife began to do the same, we worked together to set savings goals for the family. Setting aside money each month for home and auto repairs became important. We started college savings accounts years before we had kids.

Although we would not experience the real impact of that decision for years, it turned out to be incredibly helpful.

Switching Careers and Making Steady Progress

In 2001, I chose to leave my job. I had moved up to the position of National Recruiting Manager for the same company I had worked for in sales. We had moved back to Bowling Green at that point and, at the time, I was making $62,000. Not bad for 2001. Then I chose to join the firm I am with today.

It is a financial services firm created as the umbrella company for independent financial advisors, which allows us to benefit from their structure and resources.. The company has the required government oversight on all financial transactions and maintains strategic relationships with major life and health insurance carriers.

Initially, they gave me a stipend of $36,000 against future commissions. It was a regular paycheck, but certainly not a gift. When this opportunity arose, my wife and I had paid off our house in Bowling Green and again had no debt. The stipend allowed me to make the jump to this opportunity. My ability to take this job was a direct result of decisions my wife and I had made ten years prior.

Now that I was essentially managing my own small business and office, goals became central to my success. To build a clientele, you need to meet with a large number of people. To do that, you have to contact more people. I put together a postcard mailer, bought some limited advertising, and subscribed to a Welcome Wagon list of all new homeowners coming into our area. Many new homeowners are newly married, and some families upsize to larger homes. The university regularly brought new people into our area.

When people take on a new mortgage, it is common for them to review their life insurance. Newly married couples and new parents also need life insurance. People moving from other cities may have a 401(k) account or other investments that need attention now that they have changed jobs and locations. It was a process of reaching people who may have a need, asking for a personal meeting, and then tending to their needs. Mind you, this was before the federal do-not-call list, and most people still had landlines.

I set a goal to make phone calls two evenings per week, every week for two years. For the most part, I didn't veer from it. There were some beautiful evenings in the summer when no one answered their phone because of the gorgeous weather. There were a few times I went home to spend the time with my family, but not very many. As a result, my practice multiplied, and I earned my office in the third year. The company puts you in a cubicle until you can prove that you can build your practice. It took me about three years to replace my previous income and another two to double what I had made in my earlier job. I think it was worth the risk.

> I set a goal to make phone calls two evenings per week, every week for two years.

Each year, I would sit down with one of the veteran salespeople who would mentor us younger advisors. Most of the agents had come to the company straight out of college. I came here when I was forty-five. So the veteran advisor who mentored me was ten years younger than me.

Regardless, he had the knowledge and experience I needed, and he had continued to be one of the top producers at the firm. Every December, I met with him to review the past year and set goals for the coming year. It was an integral part of my growth. Regardless of the goals I set, he would push them a little higher. Most of the time, I hit the higher goals.

Qualifying for MDRT

In 2011, I came across a book called *The One Page Business Plan* by Jim Horan. I had heard of the book but never read it. It cost a grand total of $35, but it was the best book I have ever purchased. It helped me break down areas of my business and caused me to think about each section—sales, marketing staff, process, and procedures. Then it encourages readers to set goals for each area and provides a process to put a five-year plan in place.

The top producers in the firm I worked for were all members of the Million Dollar Round Table (MDRT). It is a worldwide organization of insurance and financial advisors, and they hold an annual meeting in a major US city every June. You cannot join; you must qualify. Following the beginning level of MDRT qualification is Court of the Table (CoT) and then Top of the Table (ToT). As I met with my mentor and reviewed the process, I realized the MDRT goals aligned with mine. I embraced the challenges and goals set forth by MDRT and progressed through the levels, finally reaching Top of the Table in 2015.

Most of the advisors at this firm have been here since they were twenty-two. At first, I couldn't compete with our top reps at first because they had established significant practices over twenty-five years. However, some advisors had gotten complacent over the years and were happy with their incomes. It wasn't long before I started passing them, one by one.

The firm does not publish people's incomes; however, it does offer a cash bonus to the top fifteen reps in each of three areas: securities sales, health insurance sales, and risk management, which includes life insurance, disability, and long-term care. That ranking list is made public to the advisors. Thanks to my consistent goal setting, I worked my way up the list and ranked number 6 on the security sales list in 2022—ahead of many advisors who have many more years of experience than I do.

A few of those advisors have even hunted me down and asked what I was doing and how I grew my practice. I am always glad to share. It is fascinating, though, how quickly the interest wanes when I tell them that I set very specific goals in each area of my practice. I get some glib answers, and some even say, "I tried that once."

The bottom line is that they are not willing to focus and pay the price necessary to grow their practices. They have either gotten comfortable, or they believe goal setting would put too much pressure on them to succeed. Over the years, I have heard many excuses for failure. It surprises me when people who are generally successful make excuses that keep them from getting better. Simply by listening to people who have valuable guidance to offer, they could save themselves a lot of time, agony, and money.

Each of us must realize that we are not the smartest person in the room. Somebody knows something that we do not. Learning from them makes us all better.

> "If you aren't willing to change, how can you get better?"
> —Phil Michelson, in a Callaway golf-ball commercial, 2017

Now, let's explore how goals help us make much-needed changes in our lives.

GOALS INSPIRE US TO CHANGE

Many successful people have written about goals. For example, Napoleon Hill, the author of the classic, best-selling book *Think and Get Rich*, wrote, "A goal is a dream with a deadline." Others have switched that quote around so it says, "A goal without a deadline is just a dream."

Dreams and goals are not the same. In my estimation, a *dream* is the thought of what we would like to accomplish or have for our family, whereas a *goal* is a step in the process of achieving that dream. Many people dream. Not as many set goals to accomplish those dreams.

Both dreams and goals are critical to *getting there*—wherever you are trying to go. And, while goals involve a lot more than dreams, they do need to *begin* with dreams. Dreams give us a reason to set goals.

The Power of Goals

If you are a sports fan, especially of team sports, you know how important goals are. In hockey and soccer, they are called goals; in basketball, a basket; in football, a touchdown in the end zone (which contains a goal post). Imagine how boring and silly a football game would be if the teams did not know which end zone they were aiming for.

Imagine how ridiculous the game would be if each team could take the most accessible path to an end zone. The quarterback would run backward with no one in his way. The intercepted pass would be taken in the same direction the opposition was going if it was the easier end zone to get into. Football would not be the national pastime it has become if this were the case.

Because each team must reach opposing end zones to score, outmaneuvering their opponents along the way, they need strategy, strength, and agility, all working together to achieve the goal. Also, they must have strategy, strength, and power on defense as they try to keep the opposing team from the target.

In football and many other sports, the ultimate objective is not to reach the goal—it's to win. To win, you must achieve the goal more times than your opponent. In life, the objective is not just to accomplish your goals but to reach as many goals as you can so you can live the kind of life you desire.

We have all heard the story of people who were lost at sea or lost in the jungle, and by some miracle, found their way to safety. Afterward, in almost every instance, the person is asked this question in an interview: "What kept you going all those days and nights when you didn't know if you were going to make it?"

Inevitably, the hero says he or she focused on one thing. Many focused on seeing their families again, others trusted in God, yet others kept their eyes on a real or imagined horizon as they inched closer to the end of the journey.

In these cases, and in most other instances in which people have a focused goal, they seem to look far past the circumstances at hand and keep looking forward to the reward. The person in the jungle has made a mental decision not to focus on the forest, the heat, or the steepness of the climb. Instead, he or she adopts a mindset that every step forward is one step closer to the desired end.

The same happens when you have goals in your life. Having specific goals to accomplish in each area of your life will help you do things that most others don't do and get to a level of accomplishment in your life that most other people only dream of. The difference is the *vision*.

Goals Are the Stepping Stones to Your Dreams

Goal: *The purpose toward which we direct an endeavor, an end, or an objective*

To most people, "goal" is a dirty four-letter word. It implies work and even suggests the possibility of failing to complete a particular project. Every year, thousands of people make New Year's resolutions. Generally, within a few days or weeks, the resolutions have gone by the wayside. People get frustrated with themselves, and in some cases, they were never really serious about the goal from the start.

For others, their goals remind them of a big soccer or hockey game, with the circumstances of life playing the role of the goalie. It seems to them that, no matter how hard they try, the puck stops short of finding its mark. Time and time again, they have aimed at the goal, just to have it deflect off the crossbar, ending in disappointment—or worse, defeat. They see goals as a constant reminder of shortcomings in their lives or as an opportunity to be disappointed.

Your goals will be the driving force that keeps you focused on making your future what you want it to be, no longer just accepting what comes down the pike.

Again, if you have conditioned yourself to believe that goals are only for other people and that you cannot reach them, I challenge you to read on. I promise to make it as simple as possible, and you will be excited by how enjoyable, comfortable, and rewarding the process really can be.

You might not reach all your goals. However, I guarantee that you will accomplish more than you ever thought possible if you will just stick with it.

Dreams Are the Genesis of Your Goals

Dream: *A series of images, ideas, and emotions; to have a deep aspiration or hope for something*

The focus of this book is reaching your dreams by setting goals. Most people have had dreams of accomplishing something big in their lives. As children, maybe they dreamed of being firemen or pageant winners or flying over their hometowns like Superman. As they got older, they dreamed of scoring the winning touchdown or dating the most popular person in school. Many a young man has driven by a new Mustang (I'm aging myself here) or a new Corvette and dreamed of speeding down a country road with the top off, his hair flying in the wind.

As young people graduate from high school, many dream of wealth, marriage, family, health, further education, or finding a "good job." They talk about "someday" and gaze off into the sunset as they speak. They have a spark in their eyes and a quickness in their steps as they see the whole world unfolding before them.

At this point, most come to a fork in the road. They must start making real decisions about what they will do and how to accomplish it. Those who seem to have a direction generally don't even slow down at this point. They have made their decision long before coming to the fork. Some make their choice based on circumstances and existing responsibilities. Others make their decision based on the direction they are going in their lives. Still others choose to wait, postponing their decision until another day. Sometimes, delaying a life decision can be the most significant decision of all.

As kids turn into teens, and teens grow into adults, many things can happen along the way to either make their dreams come true or cause them to be brushed aside. Many people stopped dreaming years ago. They figured it was easier to stop dreaming than to continually deal with disappointment.

Many people have dreams but never accomplish them. You will meet them years from now, telling their grandkids how they could have finished college, been the supervisor, or started a business if only life had not been so unfair to them. They all had dreams throughout their lives.

So far, I have been discussing dreams as a part of the past. In the rest of this book, we are going to focus on dreams as a part of your future, not your past. We are going to look at dreams as the things you think about and hope for now, not as disappointments of your past. We will tap into your dreams and establish a plan for making them come true.

If you have conditioned yourself to disregard your dreams as foolish because of pains of the past, now is the time to look to the future. There are exciting times ahead for you! You cannot change your past, but you—and only you—can influence your future—and you are the only one who can do so.

"Let your dreams outgrow the shoes
of your expectations."
—Ryunosuke Satoro

Why You Need Goals

You might be thinking, "I have done relatively well up to this point. Why do I need goals now?" I hear this question from a lot of people when we discuss the concept of goal setting. The truth is, you do not need goals if you are satisfied with your life the way it is. However, you will be unable to make any significant change to your life or lifestyle without the assistance of goals in some fashion.

Most people do not realize that life as they know it consists of a variety of goals of all sizes and degrees of importance. You set the alarm clock before you go to bed at night. That helps you meet your goal of getting up at a certain hour so you can meet the intention of leaving at a specific time so you can achieve the goal of arriving at work at a specified time. You need to keep your job so you can meet the goal of paying your bills, so you can reach the goal of keeping your house, so you can meet the goal of taking care of your family, etc.

> Most people do not realize that life as they know it consists of a variety of goals of all sizes and degrees of importance.

Maybe you arrive to work early so you can meet the goal of pleasing your boss so you can get the raise, which helps you hit a new set of goals.

You may say, "Well, these are small goals," and they may be if you do not need your job. They are simple goals, but necessary nonetheless. Every time you make a shopping list or a to-do list, you are setting goals to accomplish specific tasks. If you have ever forgotten your shopping list, you know how inefficient you are at the store. You forget things, make trips back to aisles you have passed, and buy things that aren't on your list just because they look good. If you have also forgotten your coupons, this little misdirection in your life has just cost you money.

This situation in itself is not a crisis, but imagine how your food bill would grow if you *never* shopped with a list. You would constantly be out of the food you need and have too much of the food you do not need. Besides, you would not be able to take advantage of specials and coupons because you have neglected to plan.

If you have ever planned a formal wedding or large event, you already have an appreciation for planning. Can you imagine what the wedding day would be like if there were no coordinated planning? Imagine the chaos that might ensue. The custodian shows up late to open the hall, and there is a leftover mess from the party that went on the previous night. The photographer, florist, organist, and pastor show up whenever they think it's time. The groomsmen and bridesmaids wear whatever they think is appropriate. I doubt if there would be the elegant dresses in matching colors that are standard at most weddings.

The caterers fix whatever food they think you would like and bill you accordingly. Because there was no planning, they do not have a limit on their budget. I would not want to get that bill! The DJ or band shows up when they like and play whatever songs they know. Because there was no planning, you did not specify that you wanted popular music. This band knows only polkas.

The bartender pours cocktails in water glasses because he does not have any limits, and he chooses the best champagne because it makes his boss happy. Plus, there is no one scheduled to clean up after the reception, so the parents have to stay well past midnight.

This does not sound to me like a wedding day to remember.

I think by now you've gotten the point. You need goals to help you get the most out of your life. You have dreams and desires that are deep inside you, just waiting to get out. You can go through the rest of your life without a "shopping list," but you will pay a much higher price for everything along the way. You can go along without planning the next major event in your life, but it may turn out to be a time you want to forget instead of a time to remember. A lack of goals in your life will not kill you or harm you, but when you get to the end of the road and look back at where you could have gone, it may disappoint you.

When You Achieve a Goal, Set a New One

One of the unique aspects of getting older is that, hopefully, you begin achieving some of those goals you've had for years. Maybe you've sent your kids to college and can pay for a good portion of it. Maybe you have taken that dream vacation or now have the house you always wanted. As you begin to check some items off your bucket list, it is an exciting feeling.

Setting and striving toward goals is an ongoing process. Once you achieve one goal, it's time to set another one!

While you can sit back and enjoy the fruits of your hard work and planning, you also realize that you are getting older and do not have as much time as you did when you were young. That awareness of time passing has given me an increased desire to complete some of those goals that have languished over the years. They were on my "someday" list but were never real goals. It is now important for me to figure out which of those hopes and dreams are essential.

> That awareness of time passing has given me an increased desire to complete some of those goals that have languished over the years.

I believe we always need to set goals, accomplish them, and then set *new* goals and work toward accomplishing them. This keeps us moving forward, and it keeps us focused on *getting there.*

GOALS HELP YOU HARNESS YOUR VISION AND PURPOSE

Many people have lived their entire lives with no concept of their vision or purpose. They know God must have put them on this Earth for some reason, but they were so busy living their day-to-day lives that they never explored what that reason is. Having a vision keeps you forward-focused and prevents you from wandering aimlessly through life.

Vision: The Power of Direction

Vision: *Intelligent foresight, a mental image produced by the imagination, something seen or conceived in one's mind*

If you have studied historical figures of the industrial age, most of them were considered visionaries. For some reason, they had the ability to conceive ideas in their minds and then become determined to move toward them. For example, Thomas Edison must have had a clear vision of what he was trying to accomplish if he was willing to try more than ten thousand times before he made the electric lightbulb work. Henry Ford envisioned a nation moving about on a "horseless carriage" and pushed to make that vision come true.

More recent visionaries are people like Steve Jobs. He envisioned people working from home with the power of computers. Then he dreamed of the ability of carrying an entire record or tape collection in a device that fits in the palm of your hand.

Michelangelo did not have a model or a picture to copy when he painted the ceiling of the Sistine Chapel. It was all conceived in his head. But to him, it was just as clear as if it were a picture.

You might say, "You mean to tell me I can be a visionary like Henry Ford, Steve Jobs, and Michelangelo?" The answer is a qualified yes! I am not suggesting that you will become a great visionary who is studied in history in the future, although that is possible. I am suggesting, however, that you, and only you, have the ability and knowledge to be the visionary for your own life.

Have you ever built anything from scratch or drawn a picture with no models, no directions, and no images to copy? If so, you envisioned what you wanted to end up with. The vision in your mind, your knowledge, and your strength worked together to build or draw the final object. You knew when it was complete because it matched the picture you had in your mind before you ever started.

> You, and only you, have the ability and knowledge to be the visionary for your own life.

If you do not think mental images affect people, sit down and watch an evening of television. I remember watching TV late at night with a friend many years ago when a pizza commercial came on. We hadn't been thinking of pizza at all, but once we saw the people in the commercial pulling hot, cheesy slices from the pie, we just had to have one. We were unable to get pizza at that late hour, but it did not stop us from raiding the fridge. It planted a seed and made a suggestion that our minds grabbed onto.

Every day, companies spend vast amounts of time and money creating and airing TV and print ads that focus on how America wants to look. They show a shapely male or female model working out at the gym or walking along the beach. The image they hope to leave with you is this: "If I do what they are doing, with the product they are using, I will end up looking just like them."

In the current health-conscious millennium, this one thought alone has accounted for a billion-dollar industry in health food, home exercise equipment, and exercise centers—hence those famous infomercials. They assure you that these products will assist you in meeting the goal that the media planted firmly in your mind.

Once you determine what you want to do or what you want to be, you need to envision what you will look or feel like when you finish. Then you will need to set your mind, your knowledge, and your strength toward reaching it.

Setting and reaching your goals will help you stay focused on the vision of your future. Because you are focused on your goals, and the way they will improve your life, the details and the circumstances of each day will not distract you. You now see things differently. The areas that were stumbling blocks in your past are now stepping-stones to your future.

> The areas that were stumbling blocks in your past are now stepping-stones to your future.

One of the first steps you have taken to meet your goals and change your life was to start reading this book. Many additional steps follow, but may I be the first one to congratulate you on moving toward changing your life in some way. The future is yours, and there is very little out there that can stop you if you are determined enough and you stick with it. None of us knows what tomorrow will bring. But setting goals can give you a sense of direction.

Be an Expert, Not a Wanderer

Many people are doing "fine" in their jobs, with their families, and in their lives. They may not realize that goal setting is something they need to do or how dramatic an impact it can have on their lives. Sometimes, these are the hardest people to convince to embrace goal setting.

They are generally good at what they do and seem successful in their lives and jobs. Things are good—they get raises with their reviews, and that is how things are supposed to be. But they're not really striving for anything in particular. These people without goals are wandering through life.

You may have heard the term "jack of all trades, master of none." This implies that somebody is generally a good worker with broad skills. These people can be reliable, dependable, and good employees, but they have not mastered a specific skill that helps them stand out. They have not focused any energy on becoming experts in any aspect of their jobs. Having such expertise could make them more valuable, provide more opportunity, and help them derive more satisfaction.

Because these people are happy with their jobs and lives, it may not have occurred to them to set goals and make changes. I grew up with several people who felt they had to get a job and work in it until they retired. They had no real drive to excel or climb any corporate or business ladder of opportunity. Today, many of them are sitting at the local pub, wondering why life has passed them by. "Why did the other guy get the promotion? Why are others lucky when I'm not?"

People who share that belief go to work every day and provide for their families, but that's it. Meanwhile, the people who have focused on becoming *experts* in some area of their work pass them by. Their specialized expertise puts them in high demand.

Here is a personal example of this scenario. After graduating from college, I worked from 1978 to 1984 for a couple of different restaurant chains in management. Those were the early years of computerized cash registers, and they were not as easy to program as they are now. My general manager approached me and asked if I would be interested in learning the system and becoming their on-site expert on it. I jumped at the chance.

I will spare you the details, but it was not an intuitive system. In addition, our bar items and some appetizers had two price structures for the exact same item—regular pricing and happy-hour pricing.

So I interviewed the management staff to understand the price structure and what mistakes our staff members continually made in the system. I questioned our top wait staff and trainers so I could understand some of the frustrations they had with the system and changes they would like to see. Then I went to work trying to solve the system's limitations. The result was a register system that made sense and eliminated many of the mistakes and frustrations of management and staff. It was a big hit.

What I didn't know was that the company was getting ready to revamp one of the other restaurants into the then-popular Tex-Mex style. A month before the new restaurant was to open, I was asked to move to the new location and was also asked to set up all its registers using a system that was similar to the one I had created. Having focus and specialized expertise provided me an opportunity that others did not get.

> **Having focus and specialized expertise provided me an opportunity that others did not get.**

Drive: A Sustained Effort Over Time

Drive: *An impelling culturally acquired concern, interest, or longing; a dynamic quality; a sustained offensive effort*

Although *drive* and *purpose* are similar and have some overlap, they are not synonymous.

Drive sometimes comes from an undefinable need to prove something to others or yourself. It may not have the lofty presence or warm, fuzzy feeling of *purpose*, but it can affect people just as strongly.

One boy's father says, "You will never amount to anything," and the boy takes that and goes from lowly job to lowly job, fulfilling the prophecy of his father.

Another boy's father says the same thing, but this time, it sparks a drive inside the boy that is unstoppable. He studies hard, gets his degree, and works long hours to pay for his college education himself, just to prove to his father and the world around him that he will *not* fulfill the prophecy of his father. During that journey, this young man likely finds a purpose and sets goals to accomplish worthwhile things. Yet it was not the *purpose* that drove him; it was the *drive*.

Do you have anyone whom you can share your drive and ideas with? Someone who can give you perspective and additional encouragement and direction? Find someone who is successful, and share your ideas. You may be surprised to find that they were in your shoes at some point and that they can save you some of the strife and pain that they went through.

The challenge is that sometimes, driven people run over the people they care about, just to get to the other end of their quest. Anything or anybody who stands in the way of their accomplishment may get hurt (emotionally). Their *drive* is admirable, but it needs to be combined with *direction* and *vision* to bring *purpose* and focus to the *goals*.

Goals Give You the "Burn"—A Positive Mental Outlook

When my sales manager mentored me in increasing sales, that's when I first started goal setting. I was not nearly as excited about the idea as he was; I thought I was doing pretty well. However, increased sales meant increased income, and that was fine with me.

What I did not anticipate was the power that goal setting had on my mental outlook. Setting goals vitalized me in a way I did not expect. By setting a goal to make a certain number of calls each day, and also to make a specific number of presentations per day, it became a driving force in my mind—a "burn." Instead of passing up a retail opportunity, I pursued it because it was a chance to add to my tally. When I would come across an interested prospect, I made sure I showed multiple products.

If I had not made the required number of calls or presentations, I would stay in my territory and make more calls. Because I had daily goals, with weekly totals, I could carry calls over to the next day, but that meant even more calls I would have to make the next day. Better to get them done today. As the increased number of calls quickly led to increased opportunities, and then more sales, it generated excitement in me that I had not had before. I could not wait to get back out and see clients! I was in a great mood when I met with prospects, and they fed off that excitement. It impacted every aspect of my day.

I took shorter lunch breaks so I could make more calls. My calls became more successful as my confidence grew. It had a dramatic impact on my career.

Although I have found that setting goals is very effective, I have also seen that setting goals *with a purpose* is dramatically more effective. If you can set a goal that has an emotional reason, that is the most effective type of goal.

"Winners make a habit of manufacturing their own positive expectations in advance of the event."
—Brian Tracy

A Lifetime Battle with Weight, Spanning Generations

Earlier, I mentioned that my dad struggled with his weight. In fact, most of the men in my family were overweight—not obese; just heavier than they needed to be. They didn't see it as a problem, though. Instead, the men in my family seemed to take pride in their size. So as I grew up, I was heavier than I should have been, but my physique and weight seemed normal. I could dress well and buy appropriate clothing, so it did not seem to be an issue.

As an adult, I lost weight several times—sometimes very successfully, losing thirty to forty pounds on a specific diet plan. Unfortunately, I always put the weight back on over the next couple years. Though I wanted to be thinner, my mental picture of myself was as a larger man.

Fast-forward thirty years. I watched my father struggle with being overweight his entire life. Because my dad never took care of himself, he struggled with continual health issues and died at the early age of sixty-three. Yet surprisingly, losing my dad prematurely still did not have an impact on my weight or lifestyle.

My wife and I got married and started a family later in life. Being an older dad, I needed to be active with my kids well into my sixties. Somewhere around my fifty-seventh birthday, I realized I would be sixty soon, and then sixty-three—the age at which my dad passed. The thought of not being there for my family really scared me. I decided to make a change.

I searched out a weight-loss program that had been successful for a friend, signed up for the program, and began to make the changes recommended. The result was that I dropped sixty-five pounds, bought a new wardrobe, and continued to live a much healthier lifestyle. I still struggle with my weight, but because I am motivated by a specific purpose—to be around for my family—it is much easier to embrace the lifestyle I need to follow to remain healthy.

Does this guarantee a longer life? No, but chances are, I will live a longer and healthier life because of the changes I have made. Having that driving reason can make all the difference. It did for me! But it didn't happen until I clarified my vision and purpose.

Harness the Power—Like Niagara Falls

So far, we have touched on many personality traits that may have a positive or negative aspect on your surroundings and the people you love. All of them have the ability to inspire change. I think it becomes quite evident that there needs to be a focus, direction, and vision attached to your goals if you want to effect positive change and still be loved by those around you.

Every year, my family crosses through Niagara Falls on our way to our Canadian cottage. We have stopped many times over the years, sometimes standing and watching, other times taking the *Maid of the Mist* boat ride near the turbulent waterfalls. Regardless of how we visit this wonder of the world, we are always left in awe by its size, volume of water, and the immense power the water creates as it tumbles over the falls.

The water in those falls has flowed for hundreds or thousands of years, passing over the falls and falling below into a quiet pool. It is a beautiful sight.

In 1893, Nikola Tesla and George Westinghouse built the first hydroelectric power plant at Niagara Falls to drive electricity to the states and towns nearby, finally harnessing the power of this beautiful sight.[1]

1. "How Nikola Tesla Harnessed the Power of Niagara Falls," United States Society on Dams (USSD), date unknown, https://www.ussdams.org/our-news/how-nikola-tesla-harnessed-the-power-of-niagara-falls/.

Today, the Niagara Power Project is New York State's biggest producer of electricity, providing up to 2.6 million kilowatts of clean electricity generated by two facilities—the Robert Moses Niagara Power Plant and the Lewiston Pump Generating Plant. The Niagara Power Project uses a gated tunnel under the City of Niagara to divert water from the Niagara River into two reservoirs. Releasing water from the reservoirs creates the power. When the Niagara plant produced its first power in 1961, it was the largest hydropower facility in the Western world. President John F. Kennedy called it "an example to the world of North American efficiency and determination."[2]

Did this development change the river and what it does? I am sure, in some ways, it did. However, this great river continues to flow, with its power harnessed for the benefit of millions.

Whatever your drive, whatever your purpose, I want to help you harness that power in your life for the betterment of yourself, your family, and those around you.

> I want to help you harness that power in your life for the betterment of yourself, your family, and those around you.

The Key to Failure

I am not going to pretend to know what the key to success is. There are many aspects to it, and volumes of books have been written on the subject.

However, I do know what the key to failure is. In my experience, the foundation of failure is *not knowing that there is a key to success.*

I believe the key to success is different for everybody. However, the key to failure is the same.

2. "The Niagara Power Project: Providing Power for NY," New York State website, date unknown, https://www.nypa.gov/power/generation/niagara-power-project.

Of course, if you are lazy and just don't show up to school or work, you are going to fail. I am talking about the people who *do* show up for school or work every day. They do their job, take their breaks, go home and eat dinner, watch TV and the news, and then go to bed. They get up the next day and do it all over again.

You may say, "Well, that's life!" However, I think it is the path to failure. Taking what life hands you at face value is a way to *survive*, but I don't feel it is a way to *live*! You may think you have limited skills or that you are not that bright. You may have a hard time learning new things. That may be true, but that is not an excuse not to try to improve your life.

> Taking what life hands you at face value is a way to survive, but I don't feel it is a way to *live*!

Is there an opportunity at work to assist your supervisor with a project? Is there an opportunity to learn a new skill, a new machine, or some necessary procedure? I have a friend who is the safety officer for his line at the plant. He does his daily job, but the company paid for him to take a couple of safety classes, and now he is the safety officer on his shift. He gets a little more hourly pay for the title, and it allows him to communicate with his colleagues regarding safety. It makes him more valuable to the plant, and it gives him more personal fulfillment.

Now, if the key to *failure* is allowing life to pass you by and accepting the status quo, then maybe the key to *success* is to refuse to accept the status quo. If that is your mantra, then I believe you will be a success in anything you put your mind to.

Also, it is important to realize that you are not the smartest person in the room. You may be very bright, and an outstanding person and employee. However, someone, somewhere has other experiences than you. Read a book, listen to a tape series or podcast—get ideas from other successful people. Realize that most successful people did not come up with all their own great ideas. Many of them had mentors when they were young—that helped.

Jim Rohn, a well-known national speaker and author, shared many stories in his speeches about his mentor. Jim was very successful and helped many others learn the secrets of success. He credited a great deal of his training to his mentor and the impact he had on Jim. Do not be so stubborn that you cannot learn from others.

> Go to conferences, read books, subscribe to TED Talks, listen to podcasts, and tap into the experiences of others.

Broadening your knowledge and perspective will make you better.

THE PROCESS OF SETTING GOALS

Now we begin the process of setting goals. Get a pad of paper or your device, and start taking notes. I suggest you keep your notes in a private place because many goals can be personal. Best of luck as you begin the process of goal setting.

Experts over the years have used the acronym "SMART" to make it easy to remember five key characteristics of goals:

S—Specific
M—Measurable
A—Achievable
R—Relevant
T—Time-based

Let's explore why each of these aspects is important.

Specific

Earlier, we discussed vision, the process of envisioning yourself accomplishing the goal. As part of describing the goal, be very specific in your description. Here is an example of how we can turn a vague goal into a more specific goal and then an even more specific, well-defined goal:

Example A: "I want to lose weight." (Extremely vague)
Example B: "I want to lose 20 pounds." (More specific)
Example C: For guys: "I want to get my weight down to 185, have a size 36 waist, a size 42 chest, and purchase a new wardrobe."

For ladies: "Get down to 120 pounds, to a size 8 dress, and buy new clothes to show off my figure." (Even more specific, and better)

This might sound corny, but the description of the goal feeds the vision of your slim, trim figure, and being well-dressed feeds the goal.

Measurable

I hear some people set general goals such as, "I want to improve my health" or "I want to be a better parent."

Though these goals are admirable, they are not measurable. What would it look like for you to improve your health and to be a better parent? If you cannot quantify what your outcome looks like, it will be difficult for you to measure your progress. Maybe improving your health means getting your blood pressure, A1C level, or BMI down into the normal range. And maybe becoming a better parent means that you attend at least two of your child's games or other events per week, or maybe you take each child out for a fun outing at least once a week.

If you do not give yourself a quantifiable goal, then it won't push you and challenge you to keep going. It will be too easy to stop and say, "Well, I did what I could." Many goal setters surprise themselves by blowing way past the goal they thought they could never reach.

Achievable

The goal you set must be achievable. It is better to set a goal to run one mile per day and then later to run two miles per day than it is to set an initial goal of running ten miles a day when you haven't run in five years—or ever. Setting a goal that isn't achievable will discourage you instead of motivating you.

Relevant

Set relevant goals that help you improve your life, your health, your relationships, and your career. Accomplishing these goals enhances your situation and feeds your dream of improving.

Time-based

Goals require a deadline. Some are one-day goals, some are one-week goals, and some are one-year or five-year goals. Having a deadline gives the goal a sense of urgency and helps prevent you from procrastinating. Besides, you will find that one goal builds on another. You cannot pursue your master's degree if you do not have your bachelor's degree. You can't get certified in advanced welding techniques if you have not learned the basic techniques.

Write down every goal you have thought of. Don't hold back, and don't discard anything as silly or ridiculous. Put it down on paper! We will figure out later where it fits with your goals.

Now that you have made your list, how do you feel? I hope it felt good to finally get all the ideas that have been bouncing around in your head down on paper. You have just separated yourself from the rest of the pack.

Studies show that only people who are serious about setting goals will truly go to the effort of writing them down.

Now that you've set SMART goals and written them down, there are a few more steps to take to make the most of your goal-setting effort.

Scrutinize

Next, scrutinize your list. Is there anything on it that is physically impossible? If so, cross it out. If you are 5'2" and wrote down that you want to play in the NBA, you probably can cross it out. If you are sixty-two and wrote down that you want to be a US Air Force jet pilot, you might want to eliminate this one, or change it to a goal that can be accomplished, like "Learning to fly airplanes and getting my pilot's license."

Once you have eliminated the goals that aren't practical, identify the goals that are just for fun. These are goals that do not make a significant change in you as a person but are indications of your life and lifestyle. If you write down "Buy a speedboat," mark a big "JFF" (Just For Fun) next to it. We will leave these on the list, but they are not the goals we are after. Many of them may fall under other categories once they are broken down.

Do you have any goals on your list that you would consider personal, internal goals, such as "I want to be kinder to my spouse" or "I want to be more patient with my children"? Place a "P" next to these. Again, they are important but usually are the result of life changes, not just a decision to change.

Do you have any goals on your list that are considered life-changing, such as losing weight, or career-changing, such as getting a college degree? If you wrote down "I want to get a different job," that is not specific enough. Instead, write down what kind of job, or better yet, what exact job you want to get. "I want to get the supervisor's position where I work, or a job just like it" is very specific and will give you clear direction. Put a large "L" next to the life-changing goals.

If you wrote down any financial goals or goals revolving around traveling or owning something, put a big "$" in front of these. Some of your JFF goals can go here. Again, make sure the goal is definite and specific.

If you wrote down "I want to be rich" or "I want to save more," these are too general. Make them measurable. Start with a number, such as "I want to save $200 per month." If you have nothing saved now, this is a good starting goal. If at the end of the first month, you saved $200, then you can feel good. If your goal is to have $1 million at the end of the first month, you won't feel like you have done much because you are most of a million away from your goal. It will be a very long time until you have something to celebrate.

Write down a goal in such a way that completing it indicates that you have wealth. For example, "I want to save $100,000." (Many people start with $1 million, but if you have $100,000, you are off to a good start.)

If you wrote down that you want to travel the world, this would indicate several things. It would say that you could afford to travel the world (and take a loved one with you). It would also dictate that you could go in some style.

No one ever wanted to travel the world and then planned to stay in the cheapest rooms and eat cold cuts every day. They want to be able to enjoy all the different elements of traveling. This includes the nice hotels, restaurants, scenery, and entertainment that would be available. It would also indicate that you would not have to be at work since you will probably be gone more than a week or two. It takes at least eighty days to travel the world (by hot-air balloon).

By stating that you want to travel around the world, you have determined that you really want to be financially independent. Now you must define what that means and how you will get there, or as close as you can.

No one ever wanted to travel the world and then planned to stay in the cheapest rooms and eat cold cuts every day.

If you wrote down that you want to improve your relationships with your spouse and also that you want to improve your relationships with your children, combine them into one goal: "I want to improve my relationship with my family."

If there are any other goals on your list at this point, either classify them in one of the above sections or put an "M" in front of them for "miscellaneous." By the time we get the other goals broken down, you will realize that many goals are small parts of a larger goal, or maybe they are not that important to you.

Categorize

Now that you have all the goals classified, let's rearrange them. On your sheet of paper, write the heading on a line and underline it. Then below the heading, list all the goals that are in that category. For example, under Financial ($), write down "I will be financially independent," if that is indeed one of your goals. Do this with each of your goals until they are all listed.

Maximize

Look at the goals you have listed under Personal. Next to each goal, write "High" for a high-priority goal and "Low" for a goal that is a low priority. For example, under Financial, you may have listed "Save $10,000 toward a down payment on a house," and you also listed "Buy two season tickets for Tigers Stadium." I hope you (unless you're an avid Tigers fan) would agree that purchasing a home is more important than getting season tickets to the ballpark. Both are reasonable goals, but you have to make choices. Foregoing the Tigers tickets gets you closer to the house goal.

When you are evaluating a choice between two goals, an excellent question to ask is, "Does making this choice get me closer to or farther away from my primary goal?" Answering that question can help you make choices that will keep you on track.

Prioritize

Now list the categories again with the headings underlined. Look at each category and the choices you have made. If, for example, you have three High goals in Personal, determine which is the most important. List it first, and put a 1 by it, give the second-most important goal a 2, and give the least significant a 3. Then list your lower-priority goals under these, ranking the most important to the least, numbering them as well.

Sometimes, you need to accomplish one goal before you can achieve another. If your goal is to lose weight and then get a new wardrobe, it makes sense to lose the weight first. If your overall goal is to get a job as a nurse, you must finish nursing school first. Prioritize goals in order of accomplishment. Sometimes you can work on more than one goal at a time, but not always.

Finalize

You should now have a list of your goals that are prioritized by category. It is time to choose the goals you want to work on *now*. Make your final list of goals. You may select the number one goal from each category, or two from one and none from another. I suggest that you choose no more than five goals to work on at once. Pick one or two major goals and a couple of minor goals. This will give you a good balance and some sense of accomplishment along the way.

Visualize

Again, I congratulate you on going through this exercise. Now you can rest for a little while before we go on. Lean back, close your eyes, and imagine how you will feel when you accomplish these goals. You have been thinking about many of these things for years but have never gotten to them. You are now on your way to making essential changes in your life!

Remember, it is not the job, profession, or project that makes you succeed or fail. It is how you *see* yourself and your occupation. If you are not fulfilled, satisfied, challenged, or financially rewarded at the level you believe you should be, then you may feel that you have not succeeded.

Your neighbors may think you have a great job—regular hours, good pay, and vacation time. However, if you see yourself in a higher position, then your current situation doesn't satisfy.

> How you see yourself is vital to your ability to grow past where you are now.

Others may think you're crazy. Most people would kill for a job like that. Well, I guess the best answer is, "You are not most people." You are exceptional and have the desire to move higher and do more than most people. How you see yourself is vital to your ability to grow past where you are now.

If you are satisfied with the status quo, then you won't be looking for the next opportunity. However, if you are not satisfied where you are, then you will be looking for ideas, opportunities, and a path to your next accomplishment. As long as you are doing your current job to the best of your ability, then there is nothing wrong with looking down the road to your future.

Important note: Do not discard your goal lists from the first steps of this exercise. Once you have accomplished the goals you have chosen, you will need to select some new ones. You will come back to this list at that time and determine the next goals you want to accomplish.

> "I believe that visualization is one of the most powerful means of achieving personal goals."
> —Harvey Mackay

Keep the Balance

As you look over the list that did not exist twenty-four hours ago, please keep in mind that you need to have balance in your life and your goal setting. If the focus of every goal is making money or accomplishing a given purpose, take a minute to check yourself for balance.

In everybody's life, there are many areas where we can improve. If you are concentrating on one area too much, you may be letting other essential areas of your life slide. If you do not feel that is the case, then be careful—this 1,000 percent focus on one area of your life may make you difficult to live with. You will see every obstacle and interruption as interference to your singular focus. Even if the distraction is positive and would help you improve in another area, you will likely reject it as troublesome, and it will frustrate you. In doing this, you may alienate the people around you who care for you most.

Discipline: "The Walk"

The word *discipline* has a very negative connotation for many people. To them, it means they are forced to do things that they do not want to do. It reminds them of their childhood, when they were punished or corrected for something they did wrong or for something they didn't do. Discipline usually came with some sort of punishment or consequence.

When we are discussing goals, real discipline is just the opposite. When you embrace self-discipline, it leads to the freedom to live your life the way you choose.

In this case, it is all self-managed. Nobody is going to paddle you or chew you out for not following your plan. The discipline must be your choice. The consequence of not being disciplined is that you do not accomplish your goal, or at least reaching your goal is delayed. Think of discipline positively, as staying on your path, a walk—not as a punishment. Accomplishing your goals will take a consistent effort over time, so you will need to exercise discipline to overcome distractions. If you decide at the beginning that this is the path you choose and "the walk" you have chosen, then it feels more like a favorable decision.

People are funny. If someone told you that you must get up at 6:00 a.m. every morning and run ten miles for the next six months, rain or shine, you would probably call them crazy, and you probably would not comply.

However, if *you* decided to run a marathon, and the process of preparing for that marathon required you to run ten miles per day, and the only time you could manage that was at 6:00 a.m., you would do it with enthusiasm and determination because it was your idea and your goal.

It is incredible how some people will embrace a discipline for themselves that they would never do for someone else.

When we hear about discipline, we often think of the videos we see of our military training, with soldiers climbing a wall and crawling on the ground. We see US Navy SEALs or US Marines running through the water or carrying a boat on their shoulders. We think about how hard that would be. Only the best of the best of these soldiers, and the most dedicated, actually make it through to the end. Once they have embraced the discipline and overcome the hardships, then and only then are they prepared to be real soldiers.

You may say, "Wow, that is a little serious for me. I have no intention of being a Navy SEAL." That may be true, but the mental toughness for other goals is no different. Let's explore another example.

> "Discipline is choosing between what you want now and what you want most."
> —Abraham Lincoln

Chef Megan

Megan decided she wanted to be a chef in her own restaurant. She had no money and no experience, but this was her life's dream. Megan found a school in Philadelphia where she could learn the chef's trade. She moved to Philly six months before she was to start school. She got hired at a nice restaurant in the city, hoping to wait tables. However, in this restaurant, she had to be a busser for a period of time before she could be a server. She embraced the challenge.

Not only did Megan work as many shifts as she could, picking up any shifts available from her colleagues, but she became an outstanding busser. She also told everyone of her plans and her dream. In most restaurants, the busser only cleans and sets the tables between customers. In this restaurant, the busser was paired with a waiter for their shift. The busser handled tasks like pouring water, delivering soft drinks and coffee, clearing dishes during the meal, bringing bread, etc. The waiter was in charge of taking and placing the orders, handling drinks and wine, and creating general goodwill at the tables. It all worked well to provide an excellent experience for the customer—great service without interference from the staff. Besides outstanding service, it allowed the waiter to serve more tables at once. In addition to their hourly pay, the waiters shared tips with the bussers.

Megan became so good at the busser job that the best waiters requested her help in their sections, and they tipped her more than the requirement. Megan watched and learned the tableside service of preparing salads and flaming desserts and was soon preparing those as well. Managers also had Megan train new bussers, teaching them what she had learned.

> Megan became so good at the busser job that the best waiters requested her help in their sections.

Between shifts, Megan would visit with the kitchen manager, learning about produce, fish, and meats. She was also learning about ordering, inventory levels, and rotating products to guarantee freshness.

It was not long before the opportunity came for Megan to be a server. She then stepped up to the task with vigor. She now provided the same excellent service she had seen from the servers she had worked with and helped the bussers who were helping her. You can imagine that she was quite demanding as a waitress to an inexperienced busser. However, she kept it all in perspective. She had been new at one time, and others had helped her. Megan made a great deal of money in the six months before school started.

As expected, she began classes at the first opportunity. However, she continued working at the restaurant on weekends and for special occasions. She had a regular group of clients who would request her, especially if they were coming in for a birthday or anniversary.

I lost track of Megan years ago, but in the time I knew her, she had completed half of the culinary school curriculum with excellent grades and was well on her way to achieving her dream. Her goal was to finish school and then work until she had $20,000 saved. Then she would begin the process of opening her restaurant.

Through the culinary school, she met suppliers, chefs, and many other people in the Philadelphia restaurant market, always sharing her goals and vision and always asking what suggestions people had. She was deeply committed to this project.

As popular as Megan was, she chose not to date. She would hang out with friends and go places, but I heard her tell someone once that she had no time for a relationship at that time. There was plenty of time for that later. Based on her track record, I am confident that Megan reached her goals.

Discipline is a mindset to embrace the difficult things long enough to make them easier, mentally pushing past the resistance of the project, being determined to see it through to the end. Not easy, but easier. If you run for exercise, you don't go out and run ten miles every six months or so. You run a mile, and then two, and then five, until you work up to ten. Then you start setting time goals for how fast you can run the distance. It is still not easy, but you have persevered until it is easier for you to complete the ten miles, and now you get to enjoy the benefits.

> **Discipline is a mindset to embrace the difficult things long enough to make them easier.**

Discipline is the difficult part of embracing any new goal or achievement that is worthwhile. Once you have begun to master that, now you have to walk the walk. You have to make decisions every day that allow you to continue to enjoy what you have accomplished.

Every time the Olympics come around, there is a great deal of discussion about the training table. These athletes have worked years to get themselves in top physical shape, and now they must maintain that through their diet and continued training. Imagine how ridiculous it would be to have hundreds of highly skilled athletes, and they were served greasy burgers, French fries, and milkshakes for every meal, followed by hot fudge sundaes. Sounds good, but I doubt they would be at their top performance with a regular diet of junk food.

With weight loss, there is the process of reducing calories and increasing exercise until you have lost the weight you desire. That is the discipline, and that is tough enough. Once that is done, the "walk" is the day-to-day management of your regular diet, in the real world, and whatever exercise you need to maintain the weight. Many have the discipline to lose the weight but then do not walk the daily walk to keep it off. This is why many overweight people see their weight seesaw up and down over the years. (This subject I have a great deal of experience with.)

One thing that helps in this process is the vision. Many people post pictures of their future vacation spot they are working toward or a picture of the car they want to buy. Others post pictures of their idols that they want to be like or pictures of slim people in clothes they like. The more you can envision yourself accomplishing the goal, the better chance you have of achieving it.

Talent vs. Skill

Many people feel they don't have the ability to accomplish a goal. In some cases, raw talent can be an advantage. However, most things in life can be learned. We learn to walk, run, skate, talk, and communicate throughout our lifetime. Some people run faster than others; however, even those people can learn to run faster if they work on their skills.

The thing about talent is that it resides in people. They may have a great talent, and they may be able to accomplish things that others cannot or have not done. However, having the ability is not enough. They must still discipline themselves to work on refining the skills, or they can fade away.

How many stories have we seen over the years of athletes or celebrities who have "great talent" but squander their lives on drugs and alcohol? Even though they used their talent, they were unable to manage the other pieces of their lives in such a way that allowed their talent to flourish and live.

In my lifetime, I can think of many celebrities, such as Janis Joplin, Elvis, Whitney Houston, Michael Jackson, and others who died early. Talent did not save them from themselves.

The number of athletes who have spun out, been arrested for drugs and alcohol offenses, or died is longer than you might realize. Sometimes misfortune is the driver that forces a person to reach deep inside and make the decision to change. There are so many stories of people who were handicapped and then persevered.

I saw an interview with a veteran who had lost his legs in the service. He then travelled by wheel chair across several states to raise awareness of veterans' issues. When people interviewed him, they commented that if he had accomplished so much after he was injured, how much more would he have done if he had both legs? Surprisingly, the man said that if he had both legs, he would have lived an average life like everybody else. The loss of his limbs forced him to face his issue and gave him a deep desire to overcome and be an example. In his mind, he would not have accomplished anything significant if he had all his limbs and no handicap.

Remember that when you are setting goals. You are not competing against anybody but yourself. It does not matter who has more talent.

> **Your desire and discipline will be the driving forces that will help you change.**

Going It Alone

Sometimes we are fortunate enough to have mentors, cheerleaders, and family members around when we undertake a goal. They will not only encourage us but can be helpful in the process.

However, there are many times when we must undertake the goal process on our own. Whether it is changing skills or behavior at work, losing weight in a family of overweight people, or trying to correct a highly personal trait that you have determined holds you back, sometimes you must go it alone.

I believe that if people are honest, this happens much more than we realize. The difference is that there is no encouragement, scorekeeping, or celebrating by anyone but yourself. Because you are going it alone, it can be more challenging to stay on course. Nobody knows if you quit because nobody else knows that you started. However, succeeding in this situation is also the most satisfying.

If you live alone, you can post sayings, pictures, and scoresheets all over the house. However, if you work or live in a group of people who repeatedly discourage you, then you might have to keep your scoresheets secret.

One of the things that may be helpful in this situation is to journal your struggles and your progress. Writing down your progress each day and comparing it to the goal keeps you focused on the task at hand. Have a quiet celebration every time you hit a significant milestone.

The Trailblazer

Sometimes, we set a goal that we believe in that nobody around us believes. This is the hardest type of goal. If your family and friends are not goal setters, nor have ever taken any risks, they may not be the best people to seek counsel from. In that case, find another trailblazer to meet with.

Let's say you are thinking of opening a specialty restaurant. Everybody in your circle thinks you are crazy. However, you have the skill, the experience, and the desire to open the business, and you know the time and money commitment it will take to do so. How do you make sure the business plan is solid? How do you make sure you are not going off half-cocked and guaranteed to fail?

My suggestion is to meet with a variety of people who have a similar experience. For example, meet with the head of the Chamber of Commerce in your town and get his or her input. Does that person think the concept would be successful in your town? What does he or she think of the location, traffic pattern, business hours, etc.?

Meet with a variety of people who have a similar experience.

Talk to your equipment suppliers and determine what they think of the concept. They see hundreds of restaurants and have a good feeling for what succeeds and fails. Maybe seek out a restaurant owner or two in a nearby town, a place where you will not be a competitor. Pick their brains, and find out from them what it takes to run the business, hire and train employees, market and advertise in your area, etc. Go in with your ears wide open, and do not be defensive. What these trailblazers share with you can save you years of heartache and struggles. By paying attention to the mistakes others have made, you can avoid making them yourself.

> "Learn from the mistakes of others. You can't live long enough to make them all yourself."
> —Eleanor Roosevelt

Because you are a trailblazer, you might not have people close to you whom you can consult. You will have to work even harder to get the correct information from quality sources. Once you have done your homework—really done your homework—and you know what to expect, then create your plan and execute.

Activity vs. Accomplishment

At times, you will find people who want to change but are only going through the motions. They get the jogging suit and go to the gym and then spend all their time talking to everyone there and not working out. Their family wonders their loved one never sees any results, despite the fact that they are going to the gym.

When I started my new career, there was a young salesman who worked hard at looking like he was working hard. He would head out "for an appointment" with his papers and his yellow pad. He would come back in an hour and say he had a "good meeting," but he never seemed to close any sales. One day, I saw him head out for a meeting. A half-hour later, I saw him at a McDonald's talking on his cell phone with no client in sight. Not surprisingly, he didn't last very long. I have said that if he worked half as hard on his career as he did at making it look like he was working hard, he would have been very successful.

I met a contractor years ago who was good at getting to job sites to begin the quoting process. However, he was very slow at getting the completed quote out to the client. He would be busy quoting jobs but not have very much work. He needed to alter his activity to ensure that he got the quotes out promptly. It's not about how many quotes you provide, but how many paying jobs you actually get. That is what pays the bills.

What You Become Is Even Better than What You Get

One of the most exciting things about goal setting is not just what you accomplish. It's also fascinating to see who and what you become while you are working on your goals. One of my standard prayers is "Lord, make me the man I need to be so I can become the man I want to be."

I know a couple who decided in their early thirties that they wanted to go onto the mission field in their retirement. Their goal was to retire by age fifty-five and then spend the next ten years in the mission field. They both had good jobs and raised and educated three children. However, they chose to live in a modest home, drive used cars (that they paid cash for), and wanted a simple lifestyle. All the while, they were funneling money into savings and retirement accounts.

They had shared their dreams and goals with their friends over the years, but I don't think anybody took them seriously. When the day came for them to announce their retirement, most people were shocked. How is everybody else working toward sixty-two or sixty-six to retire, and this couple was exiting the workforce at fifty-five? No pensions. Just great planning.

In the process of working toward their goal, they had to do and learn many new things. Of course, they had to learn to save, but then they had to learn and understand investing. They had to understand the risks and benefits of investing their funds toward their end goal. Stuffing money under the mattress may make you feel safe, but it will not get you to your goal.

They learned to make personal purchases count, getting the most out of their cars and their house. They weren't buying to show off to the neighbors or friends. They made decisions that furthered their goals. I can remember people making comments about the older car the husband drove to work. People knew he could afford a better car, but it was not necessary to him. Furthering their goals was more important.

Can you imagine the example that they set for their children? The couple managed their household to provide the needs of the family without splurging on every want, all the time focusing on the big picture. I am sure the kids wanted things, but I know for a fact that they never went without their needs being met, including quality college education. Mom and Dad paid some, and the kids paid for some of their education as well.

Track Your Progress

Because I am a numbers guy, putting numbers to goals and tracking my progress comes easily for me. I try to break everything down into numbers and then proceed.

I always tracked the number of sales calls, counted the number of new stores I stopped into, how many owners I met, presentations I made, and sales I made. I tracked the amount of the transaction and even the average sale.

Weight loss—how much do you want to lose? How about 20 pounds in eight weeks? Easy! Two and a half pounds per week equals 5.7 ounces per day. How many calories per day to lose 5.7 ounces per day?

Now, earlier, I discussed SMART goals—the fact that goals need to be specific, measurable, achievable, relevant, and time-based. There are some goals that cannot be broken down by numbers (even though I would try). That's OK; goals can be measurable without having numerical values. For example, maybe you need to improve your listening skills, so you learn the art of active listening. You learn to lean toward people when they are speaking, and you take notes to ensure that you get the crucial details. You ask questions to show people that you heard them.

After each encounter, you take time to evaluate yourself. Maybe you keep a journal and review your meetings. Summarize conversations and how different your understanding is because of the new skills. You could even quantify your progress by assigning yourself a "grade," from 1 to 10, with 1 being the lowest score and 10 being the highest, before you begin and once you've been working on the goal.

Or maybe you want to improve your finances. Some people understand the fundamentals, while others do not. You may need to get a book or two about finances and investing basics. My first book, *Financial Planning Basics for Regular People: Designing Your Financial Future,* provides a plain-English overview of the basics of financial planning.[3]

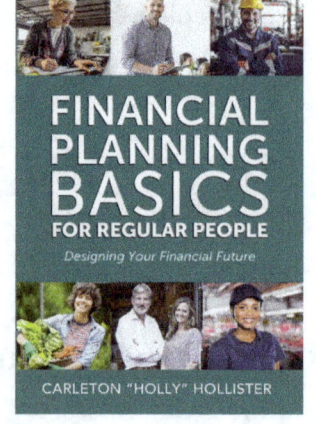

---
3. Carleton "Holly" Hollister, *Financial Planning Basics for Regular People: Designing Your Financial Future,* September 9, 2021, https://www.amazon.com/Financial-Planning-Basics-Regular-People/dp/B09FS126Q4/ref=sr_1_5?crid=259ZDDZTIBH5X&keywords=%22Financial+Planning+Basics%22&qid=1674146709&s=books&sprefix=financial+planning+-basics+%2Cstripbooks%2C156&sr=1-5.

Once you learn the basics of financial planning, you will know where to start, and more importantly, how to measure your progress.

You may want to improve your relationship with someone. A journal can be very helpful in this process. Be sure your journal is private so you can say anything you want about anybody. Here is a list of subgoals that would make up this primary goal:

1. Identify the person or persons with whom you want to improve relationships.
2. Make a list of their positive attributes. What do you appreciate about them?
3. List the things that bother you or that are a struggle.
4. Identify ways you may need to change to communicate with these people. Review each of your conversations or contacts with them. What can you do differently?
5. How can you change your approach so they may react or respond differently? Maybe it's just a phrase. Instead of saying, "Will you do this for me?" and getting a negative reaction, maybe you say, "I need your help." Wait for a positive response, and then ask them to help you with the issue. Be sure to thank them when finished. Documenting these conversations and making minor changes in your approach and tone can have surprising results when dealing with people.
6. Again, journal about your progress. Not only is it cathartic; you can also review your notes when you get stuck on a new project or issue. You can look back in your journal and say, "When I had this issue in the past, I did A, B, and C, and it solved the problem. I may be able to apply these methods to this new situation." It is also an excellent way to review

some of the wins in your life. We have all gone through tough times. Going back and reliving your perseverance through a situation can give you confidence when dealing with new issues.

Now that you have a good idea of the process used to set goals, let's look at some important characteristics of goals.

ANATOMY OF A GOAL

In this chapter, we'll look at the practical aspects of goals, including types of goals, timelines, and balance.

Types of Goals

You can set goals in any aspect of your life. A *bucket list* is typically a list of fun goals that people set their sights on to help ensure they are living full, balanced lives while they are also focused on earning a living and caring for their families.

Here are eight types of goals you can set to improve areas of your life in which you are out of balance.

1. Life Goals

Life goals are often broad, serious goals focused on improving your life and work skills to help you achieve more.

They can include survival goals. We hear stories about people lost in the wilderness who find their way home. These goals may literally mean the difference between life and death.

If your doctor told you that if you do not quit smoking, you might be dead in two years, that would hopefully be a serious enough consequence to prompt you to set a goal of quitting the habit so you can protect your life.

> Life goals are often broad, serious goals focused on improving your life and work skills to help you achieve more.

Set life goals to help you improve your work situation, accomplish your boss's goals for the department, and otherwise survive the situation in the most positive way possible. It is incredible what people can do when they are motivated—and not all motivation has to be positive. The doctor's warning about smoking is more of a negative motivation.

2. Career Goals

What do you want to do, or what level do you want to reach? Maybe you want to find a new job or start your own business because you work for a boss you despise, but you need your job to provide for your family. What skills will you need to accomplish that? Do you need additional education or certification, or do you need to be more organized? Choose goals that help you advance your career, either where you work or where you want to work.

3. Family Goals

What do you want for your family? Do you want a big house, a cottage on the lake? Maybe you have goals for your children, such as to pay for their college. Perhaps you have specific things you want to accomplish as a family, such as traveling throughout the United States. The importance and size of these goals will cause you to plan and save versus spending money on other things. Set these goals with your spouse, and with older children as well, because they affect everybody in the family.

4. Mental Goals

How do you feel about yourself, your situation, your life? How is your self-esteem? How is your mental outlook? Mental health is real, and improving your psychological health takes time. Setting mental-health goals improves most everything around you.

5. Social Goals

Another type of goal we can have is to maintain good relationships with others. Doing so is often important to our family, business, and personal well-being. You might set a goal to send a birthday card to people you care about and on holidays and call them a few times per year, which is not hard to do. It is a worthy goal to maintain meaningful relationships. Like any goal, just decide to do it, break it into steps, and take the actions needed.

Who do you want to know? How can you work your way into those circles over time? What will belonging to that circle do for you and your career or life? Learn how to network and to be valuable to others.

6. Physical Goals

How much do you want to weigh? How physically fit do you want to be? How far do you want to be able to run? In this day and age, there are thousands of tools to help you be physically fit at any age. Set some new goals for yourself.

7. Financial Goals

This is not just about income. When do you want to retire? Do you want to start your own business? Do you want to send your kids to college? Have you begun to save or invest? How can learn more about investing and money? Setting these goals can have a dramatic effect on your and your family's future.

What is your value to the marketplace? Can you improve your skills, further your education, get a degree, or obtain a certification that makes you more valuable to the market you're in, or the market you want to enter? Can you launch a venture that brings you passive income?

8. Spiritual Goals

Are you a spiritual person? Most people say they are, even if they do not actively practice a particular religion. How can you grow in your faith? What benefit will that have on you and your personal sense of well-being? It is not necessarily bad to understand that there may be a being who is more powerful than you and cares about your future. Setting spiritual goals can go a long way to providing peace of mind.

Set Short-, Medium-, and Long-Term Goals

When you get into the goal-setting habit, and you set goals for many different parts of your life, you will not be surprised to see that many of your goals take time—some as many as five, ten, or more years. Saving for a vacation may take you a year. Starting a business may be a two- or three-year process. However, saving for your children's education or for your retirement may be a twenty-year goal.

Some goals are small, however, and don't take much time to accomplish. When you first start setting goals, I recommend that you initially set short-term goals. As you learn the process and how it affects you, then you can add additional goals to the list. There can be a list of goals for each area of your life, and some of them are short-term, while others take longer to achieve.

However, I don't recommend setting a long-term monster goal as your first goal. "Over the next twenty years, I want to become a millionaire." I guarantee that you will quickly lose sight of the goal, and it will become just a lost moment for you. However, if you decide to save $1,000 in the next two months, and then $2,000 in the next two months, and then $10,000 in the next year, at some point, you will have enough experience and vision to set a longer-term goal.

> I don't recommend setting a long-term monster goal as your first goal.

If you set longer-range goals and stay focused, it is much easier to overcome short-range frustrations. The man whose car breaks down on a long trip does not abandon the journey. He gets the repair or rents a car and proceeds down the road.

With long-range goals, you go as far as you can see at the time, and when you get there, you will be able to see farther. Your experience, situation, or job may require some adjustments as you proceed. As you head toward your goals, be prepared to make some slight changes in your course. This is no different than experiencing a detour or traffic accident on a long trip. You maneuver around it and then proceed.

Life can throw a significant number of challenges at us. If we do not have a long-range vision for our lives, then we are continually frustrated and always starting over. Every challenge stops us in our tracks and consumes all our energy. With long-range goals, you may get sidetracked. However, once you have solved the immediate problem or challenge, you get focused back on the long-range goal.

Long-range goals tend to force change. You may need to learn an additional skill or process to achieve what you want. You may be well on your way to the front office, but the new job requires you to train and become proficient in the new software. That task was not on your goal list, but it now becomes a short-term barrier to your longer-term success if you don't do it. So learn the software! Now you are equipped for the job at hand, and then you can focus on the future.

As I mentioned earlier, one of the first things you must decide is that you are not the smartest person in the room! Other people have knowledge and experience that you can tap into.

Break Your Goals into Smaller, More Manageable Steps

Even the best goal setters have a difficult time staying on course for a long time. It's easy to get distracted.

A goal to lose weight may only be a short-term goal—say, four to six months. However, it may be a key ingredient to a longer-term goal, which is to become a public speaker. You must look good and feel confident when you stand on that stage. I have found that it is easier to break a goal down into steps, and then break it down further into bite-size chunks.

To help you stay on course, complete daily and weekly activities that move you closer to the goal. A man building a new church must build each wall, brick by brick, and then wall by wall.

If you are trying to save $25,000 to start a business, that can be a significant number. You may decide you can save $500 per month, so it will take you about four years before you can begin your business. That could be discouraging, especially if you hate your job. So maybe you decide to take an additional part-time job for a time to shorten the process.

> It is easier to break a goal down into steps, and then break it down further into bite-size chunks.

Once you have made that determination, then break it down into pieces. With the part-time job, maybe you can do it in two years. Saving $1,000 per month for about two years gets you to the goal. So, what is your goal? Is it $25,000? No, it is $1,000 per month and $250 per week. The term is much shorter and can be kept in the front of your mind. If you think of your goal in terms of having to save over the next two years, it can be easy not to start until "later." (I have never figured out when "later" is; I just know it is not now, and it usually never comes.)

During the period that you are working on gathering your down payment, do you focus all your time and energy on preparing for the new business? Not if you are smart. You use some of your weekends or vacation time to go to a conference or trade show where you can meet vendors and get ideas for your business. You begin writing your business plan and breaking down every piece of the operation you can conceive. And you take care of yourself and your family along the way.

Then take the plan to somebody who understands people like you and will gladly review your plan. Ask them to be painfully honest with you. Adjust and keep working. Maybe you meet a business owner at the conference who has been in business for years. He was you eight years ago. Buy him lunch, and ask him to speak to you from his experience. Most business owners love to talk about their businesses and are glad to mentor a new person, especially if you are from another city and are not a competitor. Listen with open ears! Their ideas could save you time and money.

The more preparation you do, the more excited you will get about the business. The more excited you get about the business, the easier it will be to save toward your down payment. The time goes by fast. One month, then two, then six months, and then a year. Hopefully, you are halfway toward your savings goal while you have been improving your knowledge and contacts.

The long-range goal is to start your business. The medium-range goal is to collect the down payment. The short-range goal is to become knowledgeable about your business.

The more you work through each of these goals, the more goals you create. It is incredible the number of details that arise, and the more you want to accomplish as you move toward each step. Focusing on smaller goals makes the steps more manageable, which helps keep you inspired to continue your journey. Never give up!

> "Most of the important things in the world have been accomplished by people who have kept on trying when there seemed to be no hope at all."
> —Dale Carnegie

How Many Goals to Choose?

I am sure that when you started your project, you had a couple of primary goals in mind. Write them down. Assuming one does not prevent the other from happening, determine which is the higher priority. Under that goal, list several things that you must do to help accomplish *that* goal. Now do the same for the other goals. Looking at your list of goals and subgoals, do you still have time to work on anything else? If so, then add the next goal. Many people have goals in different parts of their lives. Because those circles often rotate away from each other, you may be able to work on many goals at once. Here is an example:

- You want to be a good parent/spouse.
- You want to be successful at work.
- You want to have a beautiful yard.
- You want to volunteer for a local charity.

Again, the first step is to list the goals and prioritize them. Your desire to be a good spouse and parent should come ahead of your job, yard, and volunteer time. Your desire to be a reliable employee may require you to have a late meeting or travel out of town. However, this should not prevent you from being a good parent; it just needs a little more focus when you return home. If you skip work to work in your yard, then your priorities are out of whack. However, with a little time management, you probably can do all the above.

How to Determine Which Goals to Choose

Once you have gone through the process in this book of setting goals for all the different areas of your life, you now find yourself in the place of determining which goals to do first.

I encourage you to meet with two important people: yourself and someone you trust.

1. Yourself

It's time to be honest. Which areas of your life cause you the most frustration? Which areas do you feel hinder you from advancing in your relationships, your work, and your self-image? This is often a clue to areas you need to work on first.

2. Someone You Trust

This can be your spouse. It can be your mother because she knows you better than anyone. She knows all your faults and strong points and loves you anyway. You can sit down with a friend, but the relationship must be strong enough for that person to share with you honestly, without you getting defensive or angry. Ask them what they see every day and what they feel your strengths and weaknesses are.

Now that you have had these two meetings, compare notes between the session with yourself and the session with your family member or friend. Now you should have a good idea of where to start. From these observations, choose some primary goals to begin work on first. Once you get the hang of managing your goals, it is easier to handle more goals.

Let me give you an example. Early in my corporate career, I got promoted from outside sales to the corporate office as a project manager. I was very excited about the job and eager to prove my value.

I worked long hours to accomplish my goals and projects. However, I did not realize that, in my zeal, I was bowling over some of my coworkers. I was a man on a mission and had little tolerance for delays and excuses from coworkers when things did not get done.

In my six-month review, my boss brought some of these issues to my attention. He helped me realize that others had goals and responsibilities as well, and my priorities were not always the same as theirs. Getting my projects done was important, but it was equally important to work well with my coworkers. My goal to work and communicate with others had to run parallel to my work project goals.

> Getting my projects done was important, but it was equally important to work well with my coworkers.

Define Each of Your Goals

Here are some questions to guide you in setting goals that will be meaningful to you and your life:

- What do you need to do to be a good father/mother and husband/wife?
    1. Spend time with your spouse and kids.
    2. Plan family trips and vacations to a place that makes the family happy—not just you.
    3. Pay for a babysitter occasionally, and take your spouse out for dinner.
- What leads to success at work?
    1. Are you reliable and dependable?

2. Do you complete your requirements promptly?
3. Do you communicate well with your superiors, peers, and subordinates alike?
4. Do you spend time learning more about your business, your skill set, etc.?

- How can you create a beautiful yard?
  1. What do you need to plant or replace?
  2. What kind of maintenance does it require?
  3. How long will it take for trees and shrubs to mature?
  4. Should you go to a conference or seminar to learn more?
- Do you want to volunteer for a local charity?
  1. What are you passionate about?
  2. How much time will it take?
  3. Are you in a position of leadership or a worker bee?
  4. Do you have responsibilities or commitments to fulfill?

Make the Most of Your Time

As you break down each set of goals and subgoals, there is one factor that permeates every decision you make: time.

There are only twenty-four hours per day, and you need to sleep sometime. Therefore, you must decide how much additional time you can give to your yard and the charity without hurting your family and your work. Assuming you can balance all that, just remember, if your spouse calls, what is your number one priority?

The longer you work at setting the goal, the better you get at it. The better you get at it, the more goals you can work on simultaneously. You can be good at your job *and* good with your finances *and* live a healthy lifestyle *and* be a good parent, all at the same time. But sometimes, you must choose to read that report from work instead of your golf or cooking magazine. Sometimes you need to miss your kids' ballgame for a work function, but make sure that doesn't happen frequently. You may need to pay your taxes before you start planning that vacation.

It is surprising how many things you can work on at once if you manage your time and direct your mindset to accomplish them.

Self-Incentives: Who Are You Trying to Impress?

Sometimes, you must be your own cheering section, your own biggest fan. Every situation does not allow you to be the best, to be the first in line, or to always get the award. Some days, you must be happy with being the best you can be *at that time*. You must be willing to pay the price and celebrate in silence when your accomplishment is a big deal to you but doesn't seem to mean anything to others.

The organization I currently work for is made up of seventy five independent financial advisors, all operating under the umbrella of one company. The advisors are free to structure their business plans as they see fit. Some are

> Sometimes, you must be your own cheering section, your own biggest fan.

generalists and sell everything. Others focus mainly on the business market, health insurance, or the retirement market. Regardless of their focus, many of the reps are very successful. When I arrived, at the age of forty-five, many of them had been in the business for twenty years or more. Though I had been a top sales producer at my previous company, it was impossible for me to compete with many of the producers at the new company.

I set out to impress my manager and my peers. I set my goals and my activity and measured my progress to make sure I was doing what I needed to do to succeed. Compared to our top producers, my production was chicken feed. Their bonuses were better than my annual income. I spent time with those top producers. I asked questions and listened to their conversations. When the opportunity arose, I asked them to assist me in a case, all the while learning and taking notes. Before long, I got to go to the bonus party, too.

Eventually, though, I realized that there is only one person I need to compete with—myself. So I began competing against the man in the mirror.

Give yourself incentives and rewards for your successes. When I work with people to get out of debt, I encourage them to celebrate every time they pay off a credit card. This may be as simple as going to dinner or ordering pizza. (It has been fun to hear the stories about how people have celebrated over the years.) What's important is not the amount spent, but the idea that you have stopped to enjoy the fruit of your efforts and celebrate your success. Then you must get right back to the process.

These incentives and rewards keep you motivated. Make sure you genuinely accomplish something before you celebrate. Then buy that nice suit or outfit you want, or take your spouse to a concert, or go away for the weekend. Remember that this is a reward for your hard work (and those who have supported you through it).

Turn "I Have To" into "I Want To"

Sometimes, what needs to change is not your activity, but your attitude regarding the activity.

Let's say you usually report for work at 8:00 a.m. However, your boss holds 7:00 a.m. meetings every Tuesday morning. You grouse about it and complain to those who will listen. You grumble on Monday evening as you go to bed early or set the alarm clock for 6:00 a.m. You hate Tuesdays, regardless of how much you like and need your job.

Change your attitude!

Decide that these meetings are an essential part of your work and a vital time to communicate with your boss. Decide that you will set aside time on Monday to prepare for your Tuesday meeting. Get to bed a little early so you will feel fresh. Stop and get coffee for yourself and your boss on the way to work on Tuesday morning. Then be in your chair with a smile on your face by 6:55 a.m., ready to start the day. You will be amazed at how changing your attitude affects you. You will feel less stressed, more relaxed.

The only thing that changed was *you*!

It's OK to Discontinue a Goal

Sometimes we have a significant goal that we analyze and want to pursue. Once we get started on the steps to achieve it, however, we discover it's just not right for us. There are times when it is OK to decide not to continue your pursuit of a goal.

After evaluating a goal as it fits into your life and all your other goals, you may determine that the goal is too expensive, too time-consuming, or interferes with life too much.

An easy example is the desire to travel the world. With a little research, you might determine that it will cost you a fortune and take you away from your family for an extended period. Set that goal aside or eliminate it altogether. Then set a new goal to take an extraordinary trip to one or a few locations you've always wanted to visit.

Some situations do not allow us to follow our dreams and goals. If a single mother of three young children wants to go back to college, she may have to wait until the youngest is in school to free up her schedule.

Your goals are meant to improve your life, not make it harder. Achieve them in your own time frame.

Balance Is the Key

In Leonardo da Vinci's drawing of Vitruvian Man, the man's feet and arms are spread out, forming a perfect circle. Imagine how difficult it would be if one leg was much longer than the other, or one arm was much shorter. Not impossible, but even simple tasks would become tough.

The same holds true for a bicycle wheel; it's important for all the spokes to be the same length. This helps you maintain balance.

Likewise, keeping your goals balanced allows the wheel of your life to turn in rhythm for a smooth ride. Getting your goals out of balance makes for a rough life, just like a poorly designed bicycle would make a bumpy ride.

When you are setting goals, you must maintain balance in your time and choices. We all know of people who started a business, and it consumed every moment of every day. Before long, their relationships with their spouse and children began to suffer. With no time for friends or to attend church, their entire life revolved around the new business.

Though this may be necessary for a season, until the business owner can hire some people, it doesn't make an enjoyable life.

Regardless of how successful the business is, if all the owner's personal relationships are destroyed in the process, it's not worth it. Goals are not something you do *with your life*; they are to be done *in your life*.

The entire purpose of setting and accomplishing goals is to improve your life, not to destroy it.

Avoid Overextending Yourself

Sometimes, people don't realize they are driving themselves into the ground as they doggedly pursue a goal. It can happen so gradually that they become accustomed to having their lives out of balance.

To avoid this outcome, I suggest that you share your goals with someone you trust. If you are married, your spouse probably has a pretty good read on who you are and what you can do. He or she can look at the situation with you and help you determine if you are taking on too much. If you are not married, then ask for insight from a brother, sister, or a dear friend who loves you enough to be honest with you.

It is also an excellent idea to *explain* your idea to someone else. When you explain it to them, it helps crystallize the thoughts in your own head.

In the next chapter, we will explore some characteristics of *meaningful* goals. Knowing what goals look like will facilitate your efforts in *getting there*—wherever you want to go.

WHAT MAKES A GOAL MEANINGFUL?

To increase your likelihood of success in reaching your goal—of *getting there*—I describe in this chapter the characteristics of meaningful goals. Following these recommendations will hopefully make it easier for you to identify your primary goals.

Goals Are "SMART"

As discussed in chapter 3, over the years, various proponents of goal setting have used the acronym "SMART" to make it easy to remember five key characteristics of goals:

S—Specific
M—Measurable
A—Achievable
R—Relevant
T—Time-based

Goals Must Make a Difference

Another important aspect of goals is that must make a difference; otherwise, they aren't meaningful.

You may decide to wash the car this afternoon, and then you will feel proud when the job is finished—but that is not a genuine goal. It's just a task on your to-do list. However, if you wax your spouse's car, then hopefully you will get some brownie points.

> **Goals must be big enough to foster a change in your life.**

Goals must be big enough to foster a change in your life. They must be significant enough to make you change your behavior, your activity, your thinking process, your belief system, or your life. Have you ever talked to someone who has suddenly discovered health food? They can't wait to tell you about it. They have changed their life, and now they want to change yours. They are so excited about their new life that they want to share it with everyone.

If your goals are small and do not make a difference in your life, job, or family, then they are easy to dismiss and easy to avoid doing. They don't really make a difference, so if they don't get done, then nobody will really care.

However, if you set a significant goal, it will require time, effort, planning, and determination. Now it *is* having an impact on your life. Now it is beginning to drive change. You have something to gain by completing the goal. If you do not succeed, then there is something to be lost. You must set a goal that encourages you to get up early, go to bed early, walk, read, or learn some skill that you never had before.

Goals Must Be Big!

As stated before, it's nice to have a weekend honey-do list and cross off each task, one by one, as completed. That can make for a productive weekend, but in general, these are not goals; these are tasks.

The goals we are discussing should be something that improves your family situation, your work, your finances, or your health. In other words, real goals must have the ability to enhance your life. They must also be big enough that they drive change. If you can accomplish a goal without really changing anything, then it can't be that big of a goal.

If you want to lose weight, you must alter your eating habits. If you're going to get in shape, you need to crawl off the couch and head to the gym or at least for a walk. If you want to improve your finances, you need to stop frivolous spending and begin saving.

If you're going to improve your family situation, you may need to start by being around more, having dinners together, or taking a vacation together.

BHAG: A Big, Hairy, Audacious Goal

James Collins and Jerry Porras introduced the term "Big Hairy Audacious Goal" in their 1994 book titled *Built to Last: Successful Habits of Visionary Companies.*[4]

Collins and Porras define a BHAG (pronounced BEE-hag) as "…an audacious 10- to 30-year goal to progress towards an envisioned future." They note that "A true BHAG is clear and compelling, serves as unifying focal point of effort, and acts as a clear catalyst for team spirit. It has a clear finish line, so the organization can know when it has achieved the goal; people like to shoot for finish lines."[5]

On a personal basis, a BHAG is a long-term goal that drives the underlying activity of everything you do. Let's say that at the age of thirty-five, you decide you want to be a millionaire and you are serious about it. That BHAG will affect every financial decision, and many personal choices that you make for the next twenty to thirty years. Assuming you are not the next Bill Gates, and that you do not have an idea that is going to make you millions quickly, you will have to focus your spending, saving, and investing for the rest of your working years to get to your goal.

> A BHAG is a long-term goal that drives the underlying activity of everything you do.

If you have never set goals and experienced the genuine impact it can have on you, then the idea of the BHAG can be very foreign.

---

4. Jim Collins and Jerry I. Porras, *Built to Last: Successful Habits of Visionary Companies* (New York: Collins Business, 2002).
5. Ibid.

I suggest that you work on accomplishing some reasonable goals at first, and then return to this section later to expand your horizons. Just for fun, write down "BHAG" on a 3x5 card and stick it in a drawer where you will see it occasionally. Smile when you look at it. Later, come back to it and make it real—set the goal. I will tell you from personal experience that you can make it happen!

> "Pick a goal, not based on what you will get out of it, but what it will make of you during the process."
> —Jim Rohn

A big goal is typically a long-term goal that will make a significant improvement to your life, once you achieve it.

To some people, a big goal is getting the proper education, which leads to the job they need to take care of their family. To others, it is fighting a personal "demon" or bad habit that has plagued them since childhood. Assuming we are not talking about changes that would require a licensed counselor, these changes can be more difficult than you might think.

For some, getting the home of their dreams is a big goal. For others, it's retiring to a specific part of the world. For most, it is trying to change a specific aspect of their lives that they believe is holding them back in some manner. Everybody has their own focus and direction.

For a person trying to lose weight, change their angry outbursts, overcome shyness, or dig out of a mountain of debt, these are not big goals, but humongous goals, at least in their minds. It requires changing a mindset or behavior they find unfavorable, unacceptable, or a hurdle to their future. It has become so significant in their lives that they are willing to do almost anything to change things.

Assuming we are talking about personal improvement, only you can determine how big the goal is. It may not seem like a big goal to someone else, but to you, it is the most significant thing you are working toward. As we proceed through the process, I believe you will see a way to get these goals into perspective so they do not seem quite as overwhelming.

Big Goals Create Excitement Needed for Accomplishment

The process of setting goals is more motivating if there is excitement attached to the goal. A couple who dreams of buying a larger home envisions the kids playing in the backyard and having enough room to entertain guests. The more they think about it, the more excited they get, and the more critical the goal becomes for the family lifestyle. The greater the excitement, the easier it is to stay on task, and the more buy-in the participants have.

Each person is different. Some get excited and then set the goal. Others set the target, and then that builds excitement toward achieving the result. When you are doing your best, and working hard toward a goal, it is hard not to get excited. Regardless, the joy of anticipation can be an essential driver in the goal-setting process. Here are some of the positive outcomes people often envision when setting goals:

1. **Weight loss:** I am excited to look good in clothes and not be embarrassed about the way I look in family pictures.
2. **Finances:** I am excited not to have creditors call. I am also excited to have my finances under control and have the freedom to do what I want, instead of paying off bills.

3. **Home ownership:** I am excited to have room for the kids, space to entertain, a backyard where we can play ball, trees to climb, and grass to mow.

4. **Business:** I am excited to run my own business, make my own decisions, employ others, and increase my income.

5. **Relationships:** I am excited to see how many people I meet and where those friendships take me.

"Make no small plans, for they have
no capacity to stir men's souls."
—Zig Ziglar

Can a Goal Be Too Big?

I suppose you can make a case that a goal can never be too big. If you are 5'7", then you probably won't make it in the NBA. But that doesn't mean you won't! At just 5'6", Spud Webb won the 1986 NBA Slam Dunk Contest despite being one of the shortest players in NBA history. In the 1994–95 season, Webb led the NBA in free throw percentage at 93.4 percent.[6] He set a BHAG to excel in the NBA, and he achieved it.

However, reality has a way of reducing our chances of success in some situations. If you are LeBron James, who is 6'9", you probably are not going to make it as a professional jockey. You would need a big horse, and I am not sure it would be very fast.

Once you take physical limitations out of the picture, then you can reach for the stars with your dreams and your goals. Yet you want to set goals that are realistic and reachable. A woman

---

6. "Atlanta Hawks Legend Spud Webb Turns 59," Pat Benson, FanNation, July 13, 2022, https://www.si.com/nba/hawks/news/atlanta-hawks-legend-spud-webb-turns-59.

might say, "I want to have the largest chain of specialty coffee shops in the nation," yet she hasn't even opened her first shop yet. She needs to plan well and execute many action steps to achieve her goal. Though not impossible, it is an unreal expectation for her at this time. It would be a good idea for her to have one successful store before trying to take over the coffee world.

She needs to spend her time working on her business plan, marketing, and sorting out the details of her business. She can dream about having locations worldwide, but without one successful store, the rest is probably a waste of time. Once the first store is opened and operating well, then she can open a second store.

I have watched many successful businesses get in trouble as they expand to a second or third location. Maybe the traffic is different. Now the owner can't oversee every detail, so she needs to hire a manager. Now she is spending more on labor than in the first store. Let's assume that she is successful opening the second and third location. She must provide benefits for employees so she can keep the qualified people she hires. The dream is still alive, but the day-to-day effort requires a great deal more than staring at the ceiling and dreaming.

Now, if her business is more successful than anyone expected from her, is it necessary for her to have the "largest chain of specialty coffee shops in the nation"? I don't think so. She is more successful than she ever dreamed and busier than she has ever been.

She knows the national chains are larger, but she is establishing her niche. Once she owns the most prominent independent chain of specialty coffee stores in the city, she begins to expand. With every expansion brings additional change. She builds relationships with suppliers, who give her priority shipping and better pricing because she is buying in volume. Now it makes sense to imprint her coffee cups with her logo because she is buying more product.

She must now delegate and hire additional help and managers. She can't be in every place at once. So she creates policies and procedures to train employees so they can provide a consistent product and service at each location.

Though it was fun for her to sit and dream, I am quite sure that she never imagined the eighty-hour workweeks, the sleepless nights, and all the details she would need to take care of. I am also sure she never gave a thought to the fact that, through it all, she would become an entirely different person. She would have to learn skills she didn't even know about and overcome challenges that she never thought of.

The business was the dream, but her new life was the goal. The idea was hers initially, but it took on a life of its own. This is the nature of growth—after a while, you must go along with the changes because you and the dream are one.

> This is the nature of growth—after a while, you must go along with the changes because you and the dream are one.

I have a friend who was a manager for a small company. He was known for making grand statements regarding the position of the company. He would phrase it in a way so it would be a true statement: "We are the biggest company producing XYZ in the county!" The next time, it was in northwest Ohio, and then it was in the state. Ironically, as the company and his position grew, he became one of the largest producers of a specialized product in the world.

He never gave up on the goal. He just kept rephrasing it to make sure it was true. As I started my career in financial services, he would often use those phrases about my practice, describing it in terms that made me feel successful. It was just banter among friends, and it may or may not have been true, but it was sure fun to hear him say it. The point is, he kept building me up as my practice grew. There was no doubt in his mind that I was going to make it. His encouragement further fueled my desire and ability to succeed.

Goals Must Be Written

I know many people have goals in their heads, but they never take the vital step of committing them to paper. When you ask them about their progress, they generally say they have the goal in their minds, and it doesn't really need to be written down to count or be important.

My experience shows that this is not true. Agreed, some people have an inside burn that drives them, but that is not the norm. The process of analyzing your goals and then, once finalized, writing them down is the key ingredient to the success of goal setting. In writing your goals down, you have now made them known to the world, to the universe. There is a record of your goals. Even if you do not show them to anyone, there is a written record. The record makes them real, and for many people, this makes them scarier. They think, "If I don't reach the goal, someone can see that I failed. I wrote the goal down and didn't achieve it. There is now proof."

First, give yourself a break. Be a little easier on yourself. The big, ugly world is not looking over your shoulder, waiting to humiliate you if you do not complete your goals.

The truth is, you have made a genuine commitment to yourself. Have your goals written where you can view them every day. Remind yourself of what you have planned for your life, and you can make decisions every day to move toward the goal.

For example, you may decide you want to lose some weight. Many people make a decision and stick to it for a few days. But then the goal disappears, like a leaf in the wind. Most New Year's resolutions are like that. Someone makes a statement about changing something but never really commits to the process. They may buy a gym membership and quit going after the first month.

Make your goal more specific, and write it down: "I am going to lose twenty pounds!" Write it on a 3"x5" card. Put it in your wallet and/or post in on your bathroom mirror. Every day you see the goal, and it reminds you of what you want to accomplish. Maybe you post a large copy on the refrigerator or snack cupboard. It will be easy to see when you get the munchies.

With your goal always in the front of your mind, it is much easier to make the right decisions. You go out to lunch with friends, and you order the salad instead of the burger and fries. You go to the store, and you purchase healthy meal options instead of the processed foods you bought in the past. Committing the goal to paper helps you stay true to the goal. You would hate it if someone kept nagging you about your goals. Having well-placed reminders clearly visible will keep your goals at the forefront of your mind without having to endure the negativity of someone else reminding you. By writing the goal down, you release your own power, and things begin to happen.

> Once you gain some momentum, it becomes easier and easier to stay on track.

Recently, I was in a meeting of veteran financial advisors. We were discussing goals and the process we go through to set them. Many of the advisors had been in these types of meetings before. It was evident that the top producers were also some of the most committed goal setters. However, there were some in the group who still refused to set goals, or they would set them but never write them down. Even though they were unhappy with their sales and were far behind the top performers, they were still unwilling to set goals and write them down.

I would rather come up short of a goal than never strive for anything and later regret that the opportunity has passed me by because I did not take it seriously.

Goals Must Be Well-Defined

We are much more likely to accomplish our goals if we define them clearly and make them as specific as possible. Here are some examples of the way we can restate vague goals to be more specific:

Vague Goal, More Difficult to Achieve	Well-Defined Goal, Easier to Achieve
I want to lose weight.	I want to lose 20 pounds by my sister's wedding.
I want to save money.	I need to save $15,000 for a down payment on a house.
I want a different job.	I want a job in management, and I will pursue the education and certifications I need to achieve it.
I want to live longer!	I want to be healthy. I will exercise for at least thirty minutes five times a week. I will eat a healthy diet, drastically minimizing the amount of processed food I eat and increasing the amount of fruit and vegetables I eat.
I want to start a business.	I want to start my business as a distributor of foreign car parts. My market is owners of high-end foreign cars in the Chicago suburbs where I live. I need to build relationships with suppliers, find an excellent location, and determine a marketing plan.

The list of goals can go on and on. In every case, it requires goal setters to change, adapt, educate themselves, and usually make sacrifices to get what they want. However, in most cases, the amount of time and effort it takes to reach the goal is worth it, given the benefits derived.

It may take the entrepreneur three years to get his business plan in place, but hopefully, he is in business for many years, employing several other people. The benefits go on and on. Three years seems like a small sacrifice for a lifetime of benefit.

> In most cases, the amount of time and effort it takes to reach the goal is worth it, given the benefits derived.

My neighbor, who is a Master Gardener, would plant forty different kinds of perennials and annuals. Every week would be like Christmas, with a new flower or blossom appearing. My wife also enjoys having a great yard, so she often plants flowers and shrubs. However, she does not have the training to accomplish what our neighbor does, and she is not that ambitious. But her goal isn't to compete with him; her goal is just to have a nice yard.

You can't just decide to start running and become a world-class runner immediately. I could run to the fridge and back and say I have met my goal of running. You must choose where you will run, how far you will run, and when you will run in public with a group of other runners. When is your first 5K, 10K, or even a marathon?

Likewise, you can't just decide to save money all of a sudden and expect success. You might empty your pocket change into a jar every night and say you are saving money. Instead, you must redirect funds from your lifestyle into an account for safekeeping, growth, and eventually investment. You will need to carve a specific amount of money out of your monthly budget and set it aside for some future benefit. Maybe you want to buy a car, take a trip, or retire early.

Whatever your goal, make it as specific as possible.

Goals Must Be Pursued Daily

If you are trying to lose weight, it would be great if you could work on it just once a month. "OK, next Tuesday I will diet, and that will take care of March. I will diet again on April 15th, May 10th, and June 12th."

If that worked, it would be a very popular diet. However, dieting takes a consistent effort on a daily basis. If you cheat a little, that is one thing, but you must have goals that affect how you eat every day. The same goes for physical fitness. Going for a walk once a month is not a training program, and it surely will not get you into shape.

Your other goals work the same way. Imagine that you want a beautiful yard, but you never kill the weeds or rake the leaves. Trees are overgrown because you work on the yard only once a month. The yard may not require daily work, but it certainly requires regular attention. If you volunteer at a charity, then you probably need to show up for meetings or service projects. If you show up once a year, they will be glad for the help but won't take you seriously and might stop inviting you to events.

Determine how many goals you can handle at once and how they all fit into your life. Once you have the primary areas under control, then you can consider adding more goals. However, you are better off having a few goals that you manage well than a bunch of goals that do not get executed.

Goals Do Not Need to Be Job-Related!

People often think of goals in the context of their jobs and careers. For example, you may have a job you don't like or that doesn't offer opportunities to improve or stand out. You can change your future by deciding what you really want to do, making a plan to achieve it, and following the necessary steps and actions.

Yet goals are effective in any area of life. Many people have hobbies and interests they invest a great deal of time in. Many people are very passionate about pursuits that are not work-related. Many people at our church volunteer many hours a week. The organization depends on them.

I talked to one gentleman who was in charge of the volunteers at his church. He had a great deal of responsibility, and the pastors and staff relied on him. When I asked him what he did for a living, he said he was a laborer for a bricklayers' organization and had been for years.

Several days a week, he finishes his shift and takes off his work boots and jeans. Then he puts on a suit coat and tie and reports for duty at the church. That is where his passions are, and he is making a difference. His wife and children also serve in different areas of the church, so they have made it a family passion. I would say he is a great success.

I have a farmer friend who has a passion for controlling weeds in his crops without the use of chemicals. He has gone to many presentations and seminars, at his own expense, learning how to use natural grasses to control weeds. He has now become the local expert on this subject. He has tried many of the methods himself, and with trial and error, has figured out what works better in our geographical area. Because of this expertise, he stands out among his peers.

What can you learn that makes you more valuable at work or in your community? What can you do that fills a gap in an organization you work with or where you volunteer? What new idea or technology is emerging that you can learn and become known as an expert in that area? Failure is letting life pass you. Be a success, no matter what you are doing.

Rest and Recover Along the Way

Because we cannot entirely control our future, we cannot always hit every goal we set, or maybe not in the time frame we planned. And, in most cases, that's OK. The important thing is to set and pursue your goals.

You may be the top real estate agent in your region. You may be on track to be the agent of the year, and this has been your goal for years. But then in October, you are in an unfortunate car accident that is not your fault. Because of the crash, you do not reach your goal. Now your goals change. You must get back on your feet and back to work as soon as possible. Then you must get back on track. Is it nice to have the title of Realtor of the Year? Of course. But that is not what feeds your family. That's not what is essential in the long run. Awards gather dust. Being the best at what you do and providing what your family needs is the most important thing.

> Awards gather dust. Being the best at what you do and providing what your family needs is the most important thing.

I always set my goals at the end of the year for the next calendar year. One year, I ended up in the hospital for two weeks in mid-January. My year had barely begun, and I could see my goals crumbling already. I was grousing about this with one of the nurses.

She told me she was a competitive cyclist. She had been hurt the previous year in a bike accident along a public trail. Because of her injury, she could not ride for a few months. She said she kept trying to train and ride but was unable to. Her doctor finally told her she would do more harm coming back too soon, and she might be out longer than expected. But if she allowed herself to heal, she would be able to get back in full stride later in the year and could probably compete in the fall.

The nurse encouraged me to take the time to recover from my illness. When I was strong again, I could make up the ground I had lost. She proved to be right. Even though I began my year almost a month late, I still hit most of my goals. The ones I did not achieve didn't upset me—I know I can't control every aspect of my life.

Rest and recover along the way, and you can
save yourself a lot of frustration on
this journey.

PURPOSE, DECISIONS, ACTIONS

Have you ever had the opportunity to sail on a sailboat? If so, you know the most critical piece of equipment on the boat is also one of the smallest. The *rudder* is what gives the boat direction and allows the captain to steer. Regardless of how big the boat is, and how beautiful or expensive it is, it is not going where you want it to without the rudder. The boat would get taken in whichever way the wind and the waves take it. Eventually, it could end up crashing against rocks.

Life is no different. If you have no rudder—no specific purpose in mind—life will take you in whatever direction your environment, experiences, and emotions take you. Choose to decide that you are the captain of your life. Make conscious decisions about which direction you will go.

> If you have no rudder—no specific purpose in mind—life will take you in whatever direction your environment, experiences, and emotions take you.

Your purpose, your intention, is your rudder that takes you where you want to go. Your *why* is the key to *getting there*—wherever you want to go.

As the captain of the ship, you must be aware of the wind, the waves, and the position of your boat so you can take advantage of the wind and cut through the waves. With some knowledge and experience, you can get quite good at navigating in harsh conditions. You can't ignore a raging storm and pretend it does not exist. You have to work with the conditions that exist, but you still need to provide direction toward your end goal.

So, where do you get your direction? It comes from your purpose, your intention. Once you define your purpose, it becomes easier to decide on your goals.

Purpose: Your *Why* Will Inspire You

Purpose: *Something set up as an object or end to be attained;*
              intention

Much has been written and discussed on the topic of *purpose*. I believe that having a strong sense of purpose is one of the most effective tools in achieving results. Having a purpose can change the activities you choose to devote time and energy to, or at least change the manner in which you do certain activities.

Let's say it's a beautiful, crisp, autumn day. You have set a goal to make homemade applesauce for your family.

You stand at the sink for hours, peeling apples and boiling them to make applesauce. Those bushels of apples yield only a small amount of sauce as they cook down, down, down. Do you lament the dull and repetitive work of peeling dozens and dozens of apples? Or do you smile as you think about the nutritious, made-from-scratch fare you are producing for your family, free of preservatives and artificial flavors and colors? Yes, it is a lot of work. Does your purpose change your view of the work and make you feel differently about the effort? Of course.

Knowing our purpose—*why* we are doing something—often sheds a different light on the situation and completely changes our attitude toward the activity. Having accomplished something we had a specific reason for doing gives us the satisfaction of being able to say, afterward, "Mission accomplished!"

> "There is one quality which one must possess to win, and that is definiteness of purpose, the knowledge of what one wants, and a burning desire to possess it."
> —Napoleon Hill

Five Degrees of Why

I love talking to people and finding out what makes them tick. I like to understand the underlying burn or deep drive that causes them to act like they do or make the choices they make. Again, our strong, motivating purpose—our *why*—is what drives us to action.

However, it can take some time and deep probing to find out someone's overriding *why*, or purpose.

Sometimes, life pushes us to a point where we are forced to choose a path. I have a friend who lost his twelve-year-old daughter to cancer. Of course he did not choose the role of a parent who has lost a child. However, because of his life experience, he now encourages and counsels those in a similar situation. He has an understanding of and empathy for the situation that even the best-trained therapist does not have. That is not a path he chose, but he made the most of his circumstances to fulfill a purpose that became important to him.

It is essential to understand your underlying drive for a decision or goal. One way to do this is to continue to ask, "Why?"—"Why am I pursuing this?" Children are great at asking, "Why?" A four-year-old is never satisfied with an answer; he or she continues to ask, "Why?" We should aim to regain that curiosity!

To get to the heart of someone's "why," I like to use what I call "the five degrees of why." It's a process by which you delve into at least five layers of a person's situation, and motivation, to determine how to guide them.

Here's an example.

A young couple is sitting with a financial advisor as they plan for the birth of their first child. As the advisor discusses options for the couple and gives them ideas on how to plan and save, the wife continues to focus on college savings. Even though the advisor tries to direct her toward retirement income and life insurance, the wife continues to push for college savings.

The advisor can continue to direct the couple if he can take the time to understand his clients and their priorities. He says to her, "Of all the areas we have covered, college planning seems to be your priority. Can you tell me why?" This is the first degree of why.

She says, "I think it is important to plan ahead for our child's education."

The advisor agrees and asks again, "I see that, but can you tell me why?" (Second degree of why)

She shifts in her seat and then says, "I feel like my kids will have better opportunities if they have a college education."

The advisor asks "Why?" again (third degree of why).

She says, "I have a degree, and I think it has helped me a great deal."

The advisor pushes a little. He says, "I see you are successful, and I am sure your degree played a part in that. But so I can understand your situation, can you tell me why it is so important to you?" (Fourth degree of why)

A little irritated, she says, "Well, it is my money, and I think that is where I want to invest and save."

The advisor agrees that it is her money. He tells her, "I want to understand why it is so important to you to save for college." (Fifth degree of why)

Finally, with a tear in her eye, she says, "I had to pay my way through college because my parents never saved a dime. It was very difficult, and I don't want my kids to go through that pain."

Everybody leans back and takes a deep breath. Finally, we have an understanding of the real issue at hand. Many times, it hides under layers of pain and experience.

The advisor makes notes on his pad. He says, "Now that I understand how you feel, I will make notes to be sure we understand your priorities now and for the future. Thank you for sharing your heart with me."

You would think people "know" what motivates them. However, many times, what drives people are experiences and hurts from the past—a comment made by a parent or teacher, a disappointment verbalized, an embarrassment in front of people who are deemed important. Many times, this painful experience burns into the mind of the person like a hot brand. It may not seem like a big deal to others, but to the embarrassed person, it becomes a hurt remembered.

People can have their hurts buried so deep inside that they don't even know why they are driven in a certain way.

Many adults do not realize the impact that comments can have on adolescents and teens. Statistics show that prisons are filled with adults who were told as children that they would not amount to anything or "You will probably end up in prison." At the other end of the spectrum, some parents discourage their children from certain activities in an effort to keep them from being hurt. However, they may accidentally portray to the child that they are not capable or that their parents have no faith in them.

People can have their hurts buried so deep inside that they don't even know why they are driven in a certain way. Asking the "why" question until you hit an emotion helps identify the deep underlying hurt that creates the drive to prove others wrong.

Here is another example of delving deep into someone's psyche to learn their motivations. A student heads to college with the idea of getting his business degree. He graduates and immediately takes two jobs, saving money while he works on his plans to start his own business.

Along the way, he meets a girl. He has little time for her because he works so much and spends every waking hour on his business plan. One evening, in an earnest conversation with his girlfriend, she asks why he spends all his time on his business plan (first degree of why). He makes an excuse and blows her off. She presses him (second degree), and he shrugs and says, "I want to be successful."

She explains that many people are successful and still have a life and relationships and asks why he can't do the same (third degree).

He replies, "I'll have time for all that once I am successful."

She presses him again, trying to understand what really drives him (fourth degree). He says he wants to have nice things and provide for his family someday. As the conversation gets deeply serious, she implies that she will be gone soon if something doesn't change.

He yells, "You don't understand!"

She leans in and says, "Please explain it to me" (fifth degree of why).

He starts to speak but chokes on his words. She touches his hand, and he tries again. "When I was young, my dad worked for a company," he says. "He liked his job and was well respected. He managed several workers and was active in the community. He loved his job, and they seemed to like him.

"When I was fourteen, Dad came home one day and said the plant was closing. Within three months, he was out of work. He got some severance pay, but it didn't last very long. He looked for work for a few months, but the economy was bad. Dad was older, and no one was hiring. This went on for a few months. One day I came home, and my mother told me that my father had died. He had killed himself out of despair.

"I want to own my own business so I don't ever, ever have to worry about somebody closing me down. I don't want my family to go through what I did!"

It took the girlfriend five degrees of questioning to get to the heart of the young man's true motivation.

Many situations are not as severe as this story. However, the deep hurt and meaning are just as real.

What motivates you, and why?

Make a Decision First, and Then Plan Your Actions

You may decide today that you no longer want to work in your job or profession. However, you have responsibilities and bills to pay. Your family depends on you for income and maybe for health benefits. So don't quit today. However, today you can *decide* that you are going to start looking for a different job. Today, you can choose to go back to school and get the classes or degree you need to get the job you truly want.

Once you make that decision, it is incredible what you can tolerate. If you are working to advance yourself and position yourself for a better job, then you can endure a great deal in your current situation. Because you have a specific goal in mind, you know that discomfort will continue for just a season, and that builds your determination to prepare yourself for the job you want.

Before I became a financial advisor, I was working for a small, struggling company. It became evident after the first year or so that we weren't going to make it unless the mother company was willing to invest in us. They did not seem willing to.

In November 2000, my boss informed me that they were changing the pay structure and that there was no longer any opportunity for a bonus. Regardless of how hard we worked, or the sales we produced, we were going to make our base pay, and that was it. That was the last straw for me. On that day, I decided I was leaving that company. But I did not go right then.

From January until March, I spent every weekend and evening sending out my résumé and searching online job sites. I was willing to move my family, if necessary, to find the type of job I wanted. I was also interested in some other options that would allow me to run my own company. The search went on.

In March, I decided to join the independent financial advisory firm where I currently work. However, to begin working, I had to have a life insurance license and a securities license. I took the life insurance classes over two full weekends in March, passing the test in early April. All this time, I was still working full-time at my previous job. I knew I was leaving, but nobody else did.

In April, I studied for the Series 6 Securities Exam. (The Series 6 qualifies advisors to sell mutual funds and annuities.). I would get up at 5:30 a.m., study until 7:00, shower, and head to work. I passed the test in early May. I was ready when the time was right. However, by that time, the company was doing better, and my job was still secure. I continued to work toward my Series 7 license (full licensure for securities reps— stocks, bonds, etc.). I used my vacation in August to take my class in Chicago and passed the test two weeks later. Then it was a matter of timing. I communicated with my new firm to figure out when I would come on board.

The Friday before Labor Day, my boss came to me and told me they were rearranging the pay structure again. Our pay would be half salary and half bonus, based on profit. Because we had not been very profitable up to that point, it did not seem like a good deal to me. I said nothing and left for the weekend.

I returned on Tuesday morning, and my boss called me into his office to present me with the written version of the new pay scale. I handed it back to him with a written letter of notice. I gave them three weeks' notice and was off to my new job.

Mentally, I decided to leave the job in November 2000. I finally left the job in September 2001. A year of preparation (and secrecy) went into positioning myself to move. However, when the time came, I was prepared. I placed the rudder into the water and sailed off to my new career with the old company at my back. I set my intention first and then planned and executed my actions.

> Mentally, I decided to leave the job in November 2000. I finally left the job in September 2001.

The wind blows every day. Harness it as you prepare for *getting there*—wherever you want to go. Having a plan in mind, a direction, will determine where you end up—and how smooth the sailing will be along the way.

Plan to Fail, or Fail to Plan?

If you have ever heard a motivational speaker, somewhere along the way you may have heard the phrase, "If you fail to plan, then you plan to fail."

I do not honestly think that people plan to fail. I mean, that would be self-defeating, and unless you have some serious issues, it would seem to go against your nature. However, I will tell you, from watching people over the years, that many fail to plan.

They did not sit down one day and say to their husband or wife, "Well, honey, I think when we get old and can't work anymore, I believe it would be an excellent idea if we were poor." However, that same person may have said many times to himself or herself, or to others, "I don't need to save" or "I will save someday."

I am sure that people do not sit down and say, "I think it would be a perfect idea to spend twenty percent more than I make each year. After several years, I will be broke and need to file bankruptcy." However, they may have told themselves that it was OK to buy this item or that, even though they didn't need it.

Again, I am sure that people don't sit down and say, "I think it would be a good idea for me to weigh 350 pounds. It will cause me to have joint pain and a significant number of health issues. If I work this thing right, I may even be able to die early." That would indeed be ridiculous. However, once they began to notice that their clothes no longer fit, they had a choice to either change their ways or buy bigger clothes. Many bought bigger clothes and continued their bad eating habits and sedentary lifestyle.

I could give several more examples of how people end up in a specific situation. They most surely did not set a goal to be broke or overweight, but they also never set a goal to be in shape, eat wisely, or save their money. Not everyone who does not plan ends up at the extremes, like in our examples; however, I promise you that they seldom end up where they genuinely want to be.

Because they were not willing to set direction and positive goals in life, they inadvertently set contrary goals. This takes them where they do not want to go, even though they don't realize they did plan to get there. The thought of planning your life, directing your future, is not new. But it seems foreign to many people, especially if they were raised in a family that never set goals or put any expectations on people. Maybe they have a poor self-image and do not believe in themselves.

Ask for Help!

Because goal setting can be a highly personal journey, people often feel like they must complete every step entirely on their own, with no help from anyone. That is far from the truth. Asking for help when you need it is a sign of strength, not weakness. Seeking advice from people who have accomplished what you would like to achieve can save you time, frustration, and even money.

Imagine you go to a golf course with some friends. None of you have played the course before, so you do not know the lay of the land. When you get to the course, there are no plaques on the tee boxes showing the layout of the hole, no hole numbers, and the scorecards have no maps or pars for each hole. The flags have no numbers on them. You are on your own to figure out how to play the course. One green is far away, and another green is right next to your tee box. You can play either one, but you are not sure whether it is right or not.

You and your buddies decide to make the best of it. The sun is shining, and you like to play golf. You stand on the tee, look out at the course, pick a flag, and decide that this is the hole you are all going to play. You count your strokes and write them on the card. After wandering all over the course for four to five hours, you finish. In the meantime, you have run into many other golfers crossing your path because they decided to play the course a different way.

When you check into the clubhouse after your round, the pro says, "How did you do?" You explain your predicament and express your frustration with the mess that was your round of golf. When he asks your scores, each of you is reluctant to share. Out of his pocket, he takes a scorecard with maps of all the holes and the pars. Looking at your cards, he says, "Let's see how you did."

Likely, your scores will not match up with his card. Any attempt to score well on this course was hindered by the fact that you did not know what you were doing. You did your best but had no direction. You grumble about the fact that you didn't have a scorecard like his, and he says, "All you had to do was ask. We've got a whole box of these cards over here."

Initially, you were frustrated with how disorganized the course was. You couldn't expect to play well, not knowing where you were going. Now you know that you could have actually played the course right if you had just asked for a little help. Now you really feel foolish.

Did these guys plan to play poorly? No. But had they gone a little further and worked a little harder, they may have found the scorecards and maps they needed.

> Not only does a lack of direction make it more challenging to have a good retirement; it also makes for a lousy life.

The example is a little far-fetched. However, this is how many people live their lives. They show up at the first tee of their life and hit the ball in any direction that feels right. Then they are off, hitting the ball from place to place, wandering through life from situation to situation, never stopping to get help, ask for directions, or think that there might be a plan and a better way. They get to the end of the round (of golf and life) and are disappointed with the results. However, at this point, it is too late to change the outcome or to make a difference.

We must have a plan for our lives. That doesn't mean we plan every minute of every day to the second. It does mean we can't just drift through life and get to the end with nothing to show for it and no positive results. Not only does a lack of direction make it more challenging to have a good retirement; it also makes for a lousy life. Somebody else is always influencing where you go, how you get there, and where you end up. To me, that is the epitome of frustration.

Plan Well, Whether Building a Dog House or a Skyscraper

It is crucially important to know where you are and where you are going. It is also essential to understand the scope of the project you are undertaking.

I am not a very skilled craftsman or builder, but over the years, I have learned to do basic carpentry and projects. If you want a dog house built, I am quite sure I can go to the lumberyard, get the supplies, and build a dog house. I probably would need some basic plans, but I am confident I could do it.

If you upped the ante and said you wanted a 10-by-10 shed, I don't have the equipment or the ability to build it properly. I might be able to build something that could hold up for a while, but I wouldn't park anything of value in it.

Now step up to building a home, and it becomes much more complicated. Try erecting a skyscraper with hundreds of employees, suppliers, permits, and deliveries.

The point is that the size and complexity of your goal often determine the degree of preparation needed, the number of other people involved, and the time required. You might build a dog house on a whim, but you would not start a home addition without some serious planning, financing, equipment, design, and expertise.

We often have goals of many different sizes. Some might be as small as cleaning the garage out on a single Saturday, while others are life-changing goals that may take years, the cooperation of others, and possibly learning new skills.

Make sure you give these major goals the same attention you would give a significant addition to your home. Plan your project step by step, whether you're building a dog house or a skyscraper. Take the time to plan, research, consult, and dream, to make sure that what you end up with is what you wanted from the beginning.

> Plan your project step by step, whether you're building a dog house or a skyscraper.

One Big Decision, A Thousand Small Decisions

Continuing with the building theme, your desire to build an addition to your home would require many major decisions, followed by some smaller decisions, followed by hundreds of tiny choices.

What is the primary use of the addition? Living space, bedrooms, rec room? What size does it need to be? Windows and doors, or just walls? What functionality does it need to have? Plumbing fixtures? How will it be added to the existing home? Does it need a foundation? Do you need to change the roof alignment, etc.?

When it comes to setting goals, the same thing happens. For example, let's say you decide you want to qualify for the management position at work, and you find out that you need a business degree to apply. You begin researching what school options are available to you in your area, the cost, and how long it would take you to complete it. You try to determine what area of business you would need to focus on, based on the job description. Is it human resources or accounting? Both are important and beneficial, but to have an accounting specialty when you want an HR job doesn't get you closer to your goal.

Once you decide which program to pursue and you begin going to school, you sign up for classes, determine your school and work schedule, figure out your study and social calendar, and begin the process of completing the first semester of classes. You repeat this process until the degree is complete. Each week brings a new set of choices and decisions. One of the broader decisions is to keep on course, even if you flunk an exam or you despise an instructor. Keep your eye on the prize and the goal.

> "If one advances confidently in the direction of his dreams, and endeavors to live the life which he has imagined, he will meet with a success unexpected in common hours."
> —Henry David Thoreau

Celebrate Along the Way

In past years, I counseled people on debt reduction. I could curl your hair with stories about some people with piles of debt and little or no hope of getting out. With vision and guidance, though, it was amazing what people could do over time when they were determined.

As I mentioned earlier, one of the things I would encourage them to do was celebrate along the way. You can imagine that if you pay off one credit card, then any extra money immediately goes toward the next one. That could get frustrating over time. I encouraged people to celebrate each milestone by going out for pizza or taking a night off and ordering dinner out. Not a $150 meal! Maybe just Chinese takeout or pizza from their favorite place. Just enough celebration to allow them to feel some sense of accomplishment before putting their shoulders back to the grindstone.

Amazingly, some of these little celebrations were the best memories through the process. It helped people keep perspective and feel some sense of victory through a long process.

What Is Your True North?

Besides knowing where you are currently and where you are going, there is one more critical issue—it is essential that your map is right side up. On any road map, there is always an arrow and a large N off to one side. That is to show you which direction north is, so you have the map right side up.

You can imagine the surprise of travelers leaving Bowling Green, Ohio, heading to Florida. They accidentally head north and arrive at the Canadian border when they thought they were heading south. That would be discouraging and a colossal waste of time.

Knowing which direction north is then tells you which way is south, east, and west.

Similarly, the phrase "North Star" is often used to refer to a person's ability to know where he or she is. The North Star always points to the north, just like a landmark or sky marker that helps in determining direction. When facing the North Star, you will always know that the east is to your right, the west is to your left, and the south is behind you. Just like the "N" on the map, it lets you know which direction you are facing.

The North Star's location is almost exactly above the North Pole. In astronomy, this point in space is called the "north celestial pole," which also aligns with the Earth's axis. As the Earth spins on its axis, all stars seem to circle around this point, while the North Star appears fixed—constant, never changing.

Both phrases—"True North" and "North Star"—are often used to refer to your personal calling, your inner sense of what you want to accomplish in your life, the direction you want to take. Each of us has a different True North. Some people know what their True North is early in life. Others don't know until later in life, after they have pursued many different paths without much satisfaction.

It is vital for you to know what your True North is. Knowing what you want to accomplish in life enables you to make decisions about how to get there and then to set goals that will serve as your stepping stones to reach your destination.

What is your True North? What seems to be calling you in a certain direction?

In your notebook, write down what you believe your True North is. What purpose do you feel most compelled or inspired to fulfill during your lifetime?

THE JOURNEY

"A journey of a thousand miles begins
with one step."
—Lao Tzu

At this point, it is time to help you understand how to make this journey—how you will be able to get a clear mental picture of what you are trying to accomplish.

In any journey, there are two main questions. Most people feel the most important question is, "Where am I going?" I would say that is the second most important question. The most important one is, instead, "Where am I now?"

I spent most of my school years in Bowling Green, a city in northwest Ohio. It is a small college town of about fifteen thousand and is the home of Scott Hamilton, an Olympic skating champion, and Bowling Green State University. It sits in the heart of farm country. There are corn and soybean crops as far as the eye can see. When I was nine or ten, they built the major north/south interstate Route 75 through our area. Because my family's home was on one of the current north/south highways, we were excited that the truck traffic would now be routed to I-75.

When I was in high school, I pumped gas (aging myself here!) at one of the exits right off I-75. People from all over Canada, Michigan, and Ohio would stop there in November and December on their way to Florida. People knew that if you would "just go south" on I-75, it would take you all the way to Florida.

Many a carload of college students "headed south" for spring break with no map. They knew they could not go too far off base if they stuck to I-75. They really did not need a plan because if they stayed on 75, they could get where they wanted to go. Once they were in Florida, they could figure out the rest.

Things changed, however, when in later years I found myself living in Oklahoma. When it came to traveling to Florida, it almost felt like "You can't get there from here." We had to plan out our trip and all the junctions and directions. It became quite a task. We didn't even think of leaving without a map.

My point in all this is that you can't determine how to get to where you want to go unless you know exactly where you are first. In planning any trip, you must plan out all the steps leaving your current position and then move toward your future destination. Your current location, relative to your goal, also plays a considerable part in factoring in time, accommodations, food, fuel, finances, and the number of stops.

> You can't determine how to get to where you want to go unless you know exactly where you are first.

The same is true with goals and goal setting. Even though you may know where you want to go, before you can set the plan in place, you must know where you are *today*.

If you decide you want to run a marathon but have never done so, there will a big difference between the way you train and the way someone who is currently running in local 10Ks will train. The training and the rigors are going to be completely different. I think we would all agree that the non-runner has a much longer journey to his or her destination than the experienced runner. However, this fact does not necessarily deter the non-runner. It simply defines the timeline and training routine that the person needs to reach the goal.

As you set your goals and make your plans, we will be using the road map as an analogy. Even if you don't like to read maps, I think you will find the comparison helpful. Each of us has been on long trips—some memorable and pleasant and some we would like to forget. If you have traveled at all, you appreciate the planning that goes into any significant trip.

Laying Out Your Trip

As we begin laying out your trip, and as you start setting your goals, we are going to make some assumptions. We will assume you have a basic understanding of a common road map. It may be helpful for you to get a map of your state or region, somewhere that is familiar. In the day and age of GPS technology and internet mapping programs, such as MapQuest, people no longer carry the unwieldy paper maps we used to purchase at service stations.

However, my experience with GPS units is that they will occasionally send you on a wild goose chase, instruct you to turn where there's no road, or at least delay your trip. Life doesn't always give us turn-by-turn instructions. A road map gives us a broad vision of the journey and tasks ahead.

Because the personal journey you are about to set out on will take days, weeks, months, or even years, we will assume that this is a long trip. Also, because the reason for setting goals is to make a long-lasting change, we will assume that this is a one-way trip. We will believe that you are moving to a new city and that this city is far enough away that you will have to stay overnight along the route.

We are also going to assume that you will arrive at your destination safe and sound. The journey may be exciting or even dangerous, but you will be *getting there*.

The other assumption I will make is that you will take notes on paper or in a phone app while you are reading. If you have not gotten yourself a notebook yet, please get one and come back right away. It will be vital for you to make notes and write as you read.

In your notebook, on a clean page, write something like this: "The Journey of (*your name here*) Beginning on (*today's date*), Ending on (*leave this blank*)." This page will be a reminder that you are on a journey and that when you started out, you weren't sure when or where it would end. And then, once you finish the long trip, it will feel great to go back and write in the date.

How Far, and How Long?

After you have determined where you currently are and where you want to go, and you have the map right side up, it is time to figure out how long the journey will be. On most maps, there is a chart at the top that gives you distances between major cities. Your MapQuest printout or Google Maps will tell you the approximate miles and time needed.

If this does not apply, measure the distance in inches, and multiply the number of inches by the key (the key tells how many miles represented by one inch). Now you know how many miles you will be traveling.

Once you know the number of miles, divide it by the average speed (usually 60 miles per hour). This gives you the approximate driving time only. This estimate does not take into consideration stopping time, traffic jams, or overnight stays. This estimate could be considered the minimum amount of time required to make this trip by car.

In goal setting, you must determine the approximate amount of time needed to accomplish your goal.

If you want to lose twenty pounds, and you think you can lose two pounds per week, then it will take you approximately ten weeks. It may take you less or more time, but you now have an idea. If you have five weeks before you are to leave on vacation, and you want to look good in that swimsuit, you will need to lose four pounds per week to reach your goal.

Some distances are already calculated for you (as in the mileage chart). It is understood that a college education takes approximately four years. You may be able to reduce it to three if you take classes each summer, but you cannot accomplish it in one year.

In this case, you would find out how many credit hours you need and which courses you need to graduate with a degree in your chosen field. Determine how many credit hours you earn for each class taken and how many courses will be considered a "full load" of coursework for a semester.

Then you can divide the total number of credit hours needed for the degree by the number of credit hours in a semester. This provides you the minimum number of semesters you will need to accomplish your degree. (However, your academic advisor should be able to tell you this without any math.)

Naturally, increasing the number of credit hours per semester would decrease your time, but be realistic. The idea is to get your degree with a good grade average, not to kill yourself doing it. (Again, your academic advisor can help you figure this out.)

Checkpoints

Other goals have set schedules. If you are trying to get ready to run in the Boston Marathon next April, you now know what your timetable is for getting ready. If that timetable is not satisfactory, then you may need to wait until the next year or run the New York marathon in May.

Regarding your personal goals, if there is not a defined timetable for completion (such as the case of the college education), set a future date for yourself. Your target date does not have to be carved in stone, but it will keep you on track and focused. There may be a minimum amount of time needed to accomplish your goal, but there usually is not a finite time when you must be finished.

This may take some of the pressure off, but it is wise to set a date by which you want to accomplish this goal. If not, it will be very easy to procrastinate in reaching your destination. The more you delay, the more distracted you will become, and the less likely you are to ever achieve your goal.

> Your target date does not have to be carved in stone, but it will keep you on track and focused.

How Many Stops?

Most trips of more than two hours require some type of stop. Maybe you choose to stretch your legs, get gas, or use the restroom. Other trips may require a meal or two, or even a hotel stay. How many stops are needed is determined by the distance and time. Most people would not schedule a restroom break or refueling stop; they merely pull off the road at a convenient exit.

However, most people would be reluctant to leave without having a hotel reservation at the other end. Long trips require more planning and scheduling. You want to be sure you are sleeping safely in a bed instead of in your car.

The same is true for goal setting. If you want to wax your car this afternoon, you probably do not need to have a meeting with yourself and lay out an itinerary. However, if you plan to repaint the outside of your house in the next two weeks, it may take some careful planning.

As mentioned, most people do not set goals. They go after the big things in their lives with the same planning (or lack thereof) as they do the small stuff. This can bring a great deal of frustration and often causes people to give up. The plan is your best friend, not your mortal enemy.

When setting goals, people typically focus on the final result, and that is great. Most things that are worthwhile take time, planning, and maybe money. They often cannot be done in a day or short time period. If you plan to repaint the outside of your house, you probably will break it down into sections, planning on one part at a time: "I plan to do the west side on Saturday morning and the front porch and back porch on Saturday afternoon. I will tackle the east side after dinner on Sunday. Next week, I will work on the back area on Saturday. Saturday evening, I will determine what my next step is."

If you experience weather issues, it may push back your timetable some. If that happens, you'll just need to modify your schedule. But still, breaking down the goal into smaller goals and planning for the "stops" gives you a real sense of accomplishment and eliminates much frustration.

The same could be said for a college degree—semester by semester, course by course, year by year, you work at your goal. Many times, it is day by day and exam by exam. You break down the big goal into smaller goals that will help you accomplish the big goal. However, each step is a measurement of progress and success.

To start a business, you follow the same idea. Determine the business plan and model. What will you sell? Where will your business be, or will it be online only? Who will do the work, what suppliers will you need, and so on? I doubt that many people would rent an empty storefront, then decide if they want a pet shop or clothing store, then figure out the market, then buy all the inventory, and lastly go to the bank to ask for a loan. I think you would agree that would not be a good business plan.

Having steps and stops along the way is natural. It is even better if you plan on those stops and predetermine, to the best of your ability, when they will happen. You will be much less frustrated.

How Many Turns?

My family and I travel to Canada each summer for a fishing vacation on a lake. When we would travel years ago, my four-year-old daughter would ask, "How many turns?" To her, it was simple. North to Detroit, turn right, drive eight hours east, get off the exit and turn left, go to the cottage road, and turn left again. Four turns. Simple to her—indeed, the simplistic big picture.

Such a simplistic view did not describe in detail the twelve-hour trip we were about to undertake, but this type of simplistic view is OK at the beginning of your goal setting. For example, to get your PhD in psychology, it takes four years of college—two years for your master's, and two years of PhD studies. Three turns, right?

It is helpful to look at the bird's-eye view of the project as a whole, especially in the early stages. As you know, there is much more to that degree than three turns, but setting out the goal in broad terms helps you focus on the result. It also helps you set goals and a timeline for each segment.

Each of these "turns" can be a mile marker or can be broken down in more detailed "turns." The four years of college are broken down into two semesters each, plus a summer session. Each semester is broken down into three to five classes, and each class has exams and projects due each week. As you analyze your goal, you will break it down further and further into more detailed steps.

How Much Will It Cost?

Now that you have estimated how long it will take you to make your trip, it is time to examine your resources. On most trips I have ever been on, I have had to pay for all my gas, food, hotels, and any other expenses along the way, or I have expense limits placed on me by my company or my budget. Once you have an idea of the distance you are traveling, it will give you an excellent sense of your expenses.

It is the same when setting your goals. Once you have determined approximately how long it will take you to accomplish your goals, then you can decide the types and amounts of resources you will need. Your resources are anything you currently have available to you that will help you accomplish your goal.

In goal setting, some of your financial resources may be the money you already have, your ability to save, your ability to get a loan for your project, financial support from family and friends, assets you may be able to borrow against, financial aid, and any grants you can get.

One of your most significant resources is time.

One of your most significant resources is time. It takes time to plan a business, to exercise, to read, and to rest. If you must continue to work full time and spend time with your family, while pursuing a specific goal, time is a very scarce commodity.

Non-financial resources include relationships that will help you during your trip, connections you have in each industry, experiences in job and life situations, any and all education you have already gained, job flexibility, and anything else that may be helpful in accomplishing your goal. In this technology age, some of your most essential resources may be a computer or device, the internet, and a cell phone—and the ability to use them.

Once you have figured out what resources you will need to reach your goal, you must make two critical decisions:

1. **Do I have enough resources, or can I obtain enough resources to accomplish my goal?** If you are able to round up the resources you need, then you come to the second question.
2. **Is the goal I am trying to reach worth the expense of my resources?** If the answer is yes, you have just decided to take the journey.

Let me congratulate you for going through this somewhat brain-racking exercise. You are one giant step closer to moving down the highway.

What Is the Timeline?

As mentioned, goals can have different timelines. Some have a tight schedule with specific end points, while others might last several years. My sister and her family have a goal to visit every state in the union, and they plan their vacations to help them accomplish that goal. Over many years, they have checked off each state, one by one, and have had some outstanding holidays and made wonderful memories in the process.

Short-term goals may be as simple as getting a specific household chore or job done in a weekend. However, that chore may be part of a larger, longer-term goal to improve the look and quality of your home. The latter goal may take years to accomplish.

You would not expect to lose fifty pounds in a week, nor would you expect to train for a marathon in a few days. However, you would not want to take five years to build a simple shelf for your workroom. Setting time goals keeps you focused and on track with short-term goals, and it keeps you from getting frustrated with long-term goals.

Call the Auto Club (for the Best Itinerary)

For millions of people in the United States and Canada, when they are preparing to take a trip, they call AAA. The auto club puts together an itinerary with precise maps that are highlighted with the recommended route. They will also make you aware of any changes in road layouts and will help you avoid any areas of traffic congestion they are aware of. They can also supply you with larger maps of the area and a booklet that describes the highlights and tourist attractions where you are going.

> Contact people who have been down the road you are heading.

If the goal you are about to start on is a life-changing or career-changing goal, then I suggest that you contact people who have been down the road you are heading. All colleges and universities have career counseling available for free or a very nominal charge. Each department will have advisors who will help you set your schedule and make sure you get the classes you need.

If you are changing jobs or thinking about changing careers, talk to people around you who may be helpful. Schedule some time with your pastor or a friend who knows you well and can be honest with you. I suggest talking to three to four people who have experienced what you are thinking about doing, another two to three people who you are close to, and your spouse.

There is value in explaining to others the adventure you are about to embark on. Having to formulate your goal into ideas that you can explain to others helps you solidify the concepts in your head. The more you define it, the clearer it becomes to you.

Besides, while you are explaining your goal to people who have had similar experiences, they can caution you or clarify any misconceptions you may have. It is better to find these things out ahead of time than after you are far along on the journey.

It is also very beneficial to explain these ideas to your good friends who know you well. (Your good friends are the ones who will encourage you.) It is essential for you to hear their input. They may see some important details that you missed, and they can be honest with you if they have any genuine concerns.

Most importantly, it is crucial for you to get the support of your spouse and family. They are the ones who should be encouraging you along your journey. They are the ones who will be there when the going gets rough, and they will be the ones who will celebrate with you when you have succeeded.

If your family is not in support of your undertaking, or if you are married and your spouse does not support this journey, and they have sound reasons and concerns, I recommend that you rethink your course of action.

In most cases, if your spouse and/or your family are not behind you, then one of two things needs to happen: Either you need to take additional time and get further explanation to obtain their backing, or you must make a conscious decision to proceed without their support. If you decide to continue without their support, please be aware of the fallout that may take place in these crucial relationships. I encourage you to make sure it is worth it. Proceed only if there are no other choices.

"The most important career decision you'll make is who your life partner is."
—Sheryl Sandberg

Road Check

When I was a kid, my family traveled to my grandparents' home for Thanksgiving and Christmas, and we always took a long trip in the summer. Being a certified procrastinator, my dad would usually wait until the last minute to get the car checked for the trip. On the morning of the trip, he would head into town to get an oil change and lube job, check the tires and air pressure, check the antifreeze, and make sure we had washer fluid in the wiper tank. Mom made sure we had enough money for the trip and that all the suitcases were packed and ready. That took care of all the things we could control, and the hope was that nothing would go wrong along the way.

We kids didn't like to wait for Dad to come back to get the trip started. However, in all the years and all the trips, I remember only two minor problems. One of those was a flat tire that we were able to replace easily. The other was a little more serious, but nobody was hurt, and we were delayed for only a few hours.

When everything went smoothly, my dad's last-minute preparation turned out OK. But I strongly recommend doing all your planning in advance, to avoid potential delays.

Before you head down the road, it is wise to do a road check, too. Have you analyzed your goals and your situation? Do you have enough money for your project? Have you done your homework enough to understand what you are about to attempt? If this goal is likely to have a dramatic effect on those around you, then have you gotten their buy-in as well?

If you are heading to college, do you have your high-school transcripts? If you are looking for a new job, do you have the education and experience they want?

If you are applying for a new job and listing certain people as references, have you spoken to those people who will speak on your behalf to let them know they may get a phone call? In this day and age, referral sources are often asked to complete a questionnaire online.

It is in your own best interest to do a complete road check before you start down the road after you set your new goal. Because you want the best opportunity to succeed, doing your preliminary homework does not guarantee a perfect trip, but it at least reduces the possibility of being sidetracked or delayed.

The road check may seem minor, but it can have a dramatic impact on the future success of your goals. It is worth the time!

Delays, Detours, and Roadblocks

Even the best-planned journeys can get interrupted by delays, detours, and roadblocks. These are typically hiccups in a journey that we could not have anticipated. And in most cases, we cannot control or resolve them on our own. We just have to cope with them.

Delays

Regardless of how well we plan our trip, there can be unexpected delays that arise. Personally, if I am counting on a delay, I am fine, but I am one of those people who will drive ten miles out of my way to avoid sitting in a traffic jam. My theory (faulty as it may be) is that as long as I'm moving, it is better than sitting in traffic. It's very easy to get lost or delayed "going around" the traffic jam, though. As I get older, and my wife has more influence on me, I am a bit more content to wait out the traffic. Most traffic delays are temporary, as long as you are patient and stay on the road. You may arrive later than you expected, but you will get there, and you will not get lost.

In pursuing your goals, it is likely that you will have at least a few delays. Stay the course, and do not get frustrated. Patience is a virtue and will keep you from getting distracted on side roads. Stay with your vehicle. When the delay subsides, be prepared to continue on your journey immediately. You may accomplish your goal later than expected, but you will get there.

> **Patience is a virtue and will keep you from getting distracted on side roads.**

A young man I knew named Dean had set his sights on going to law school. He was about to graduate with a bachelor's degree in business when he took the Law School Admission Test (LSAT). Much to his chagrin, he did not score high enough on the test to get accepted into law school for the next fall semester. To some people, this would have been the end of the road. However, when he graduated, Dean chose to get a job for the summer until he could retake the exam in the fall. This time, he passed and could begin classes the following January.

Had Dean gotten distracted and just taken a corporate job, there is an excellent chance that he would have never left that job for law school. This might not have been bad; however, he would not have fulfilled his goal. By allowing the problem to clear, and keeping focused on his goal, he was only slightly delayed in accomplishing his goal of attending law school.

Detours

Detours can be more aggravating than delays. Many a traveler has been directed off the four-lane highway onto some two-lane back road to go around an accident or major construction. Your speed limit goes from 65 miles per hour down to 45 as you follow the semis down the twisting country road. It's enough to make you pull your hair out, and there is little or nothing you can do about it.

Again, stay the course. Don't allow yourself to get frustrated with the detours. You are proceeding in the same general direction and are just passing barns and cows instead of billboards and exit signs.

In your goal setting, a detour is anything that requires you to go out of your way to accomplish your goal. It not only encompasses a delay but also requires additional time and effort to get you back on the road.

Let's go back to the previous example. If the law school Dean tested at allowed him to apply only once, then he would have had to make a detour. How significant the effect might be would depend on how important it is to him that he attend that specific school. Because his primary goal was to go to law school, he then might have to apply to a different school and go through the procedure again. Assuming that he succeeds at entering this school, he has taken the detour and has found himself back on the goal road.

Most detours cause delays, frustrations, and maybe even cause you to incur additional expenses. However, if this goal is vital to you, and you are determined to get there, it is probably worth the aggravation.

Roadblocks

Larry was a friend of mine in college who was in the Air Force ROTC. Since his childhood, he had always wanted to learn to fly. He had a goal from childhood to be a military aviator, and everything in his being focused on making that dream come true.

After he graduated from college, he entered the US Air Force. In that first year, Larry was finally scheduled for the flight school he had always dreamed about. Flight school is a one-time shot. If you get in and you do not graduate, you never get another chance. Halfway through his flight training, Larry's father had a massive heart attack and nearly died. Larry was called home to be with his family during the crisis. Unfortunately, there are no exceptions to the rules in flight school.

Because Larry could not complete his flight-school training, he did not graduate from the class. He had hit a significant roadblock that was not going to move. The lifelong pursuit of his dream had come to a screeching halt. Larry would not be allowed to take the flight training over again, and he would never fulfill his dream of flying military jets. It was obviously a major disappointment. There was no detour; he had to simply choose a different goal.

I define a *roadblock* in two different ways. It is a delay or detour you choose not to follow, or it is an event that in some way prevents you from completing your goal. In the first case, the decision is generally up to you. If you decide you do not want to follow the detour to reach the goal, that is your call, and you are in control of the situation. If this occurs, please take the time to examine all the options before you quit. You may find a much tougher time starting down this same road again.

If the roadblock prevents you from completing the goal, like in Larry's case, there are a couple of things I want you to know. First of all, you did the best you could, and no one can take that away from you. Be proud of yourself for going after what you really wanted. Keep your chin up, and be proud that you followed your dream. Many other people never have and never will.

Second, waste no time in choosing your next goal. Go after it with the same zeal you did the last goal. Determine that you will succeed this time. Remember, Abraham Lincoln lost several elections for public office before he became president. If he had not followed his dreams and goals and persevered, it would have robbed our nation of one of its greatest leaders.

Most importantly, don't spend your time and energy playing "if-only" games. "If only this hadn't happened, I could have accomplished my goal." They are a mental strain and only serve to discourage. Years ago, I saw Christopher Reeve[7] at a motivational seminar. He was paralyzed from the neck down after a fall from a horse. During the interview, they asked, "What if you had gone sailing or played golf that fateful day instead of going riding?"

I will always remember his answer.

He spoke slowly as he breathed on his ventilator. He said, "I don't spend time thinking about coulda, woulda, shoulda. I only focus on what is ahead because I can't change the past. I can only change the future."

> Don't spend your time and energy playing "if-only" games.

If a roadblock in life could discourage anyone, it would be Christopher Reeve. "If-only" may seem comforting at the time, but it establishes a pattern of excuse-making that you cannot afford. Walk away from the experience with your head held high. You should have no regrets about going after your goal.

To finish Larry's story, he served out his time in the US Air Force, serving with a fighter jet maintenance unit. He could not fly the jets, but he could still work on them. After getting out of the service, Larry got his pilot license and now owns a plane. He never did get to fly the fighter jets, but he did fulfill his dream of learning to fly. Even though the roadblock stopped Larry from fulfilling that specific dream, he persevered and got as close to it as he could.

---

7. Christopher D'Olier Reeve (1952–2004) was an American actor best known for his motion picture portrayal of the classic DC comic book superhero Superman, beginning with the acclaimed *Superman* (1978), for which he won a BAFTA Award. On May 27, 1995, Reeve was left quadriplegic after being thrown from a horse during an equestrian competition in Culpeper, Virginia. He founded what became the Christopher & Dana Reeve Foundation in 1996 to promote research on spinal cord injuries. He died of cardiac arrest in 2004.

Regardless of the delays, detours, and roadblocks that may come, don't get discouraged. This goal was important enough for you to set in the beginning, so it must be worthwhile to you. If circumstances are such that you must stop and return home, remember that tomorrow is another day, and you still have the time in your life to accomplish many great things. Go down your list to the next goal, and get after it. I am sure that this time, you will be successful in *getting there*.

Stamina

Many of us are somewhat spontaneous in our decision making and will sometimes decide at a moment's notice that we are going to make a change. Spontaneity can be especially trying on loved ones when we change directions rapidly. If we were honest with ourselves, we would see that we are not nearly as effective when "winging it" as we can be when we plan.

One of the significant advantages of planning your goals and laying out your trip is that it helps maintain a steady course. If you were making a three-day drive across the country, it is essential to decide how far you are going to go each day and where you are going to stop and rest. This allows you to make hotel reservations ahead of time and ensure that there will be a nice, warm bed waiting for you at the end of the day.

To head out on a trip like this with no idea how far you are going to travel is adventurous at best and foolish at worst. You can easily find yourself weary and unable to stay awake, yet at a place where there are no rooms, or worse, no hotel. Trust me when I say that you will sleep better in a bed than in the back seat of your car.

As you pursue your goal, anticipate the need to rest periodically. When you focus on an important goal, it is easy to get both physically and mentally run down. When this happens, you will not be operating at the top of your game. This is when you might make mistakes or miss an important detail.

You would not plan a three-thousand-mile trip and try to drive it straight through with no sleep. I am sure that if you tried, you would be a menace to those on the highway and could put your own life in serious danger. As the old adage says, "Better to get there alive than not at all." At some point, you may have to put in some extra time, but running yourself ragged all the time is not going to help you accomplish your goal. Even assuming you reach the goal whole and safe, you may be too tired or sick to enjoy it.

> Running yourself ragged all the time is not going to help you accomplish your goal.

A friend of mine went to college but put his goal of completing a degree at risk because he refused to accept help. His dad had planned for the expenses and was more than willing to help his son with them. However, my friend was bound and determined to pay for everything himself. He signed up for a full load of classes and worked three-part time jobs.

After the first semester, he had not done very well, and his dad again offered to help with the expenses. He told his son that if wanted to pay him back at a later time, he would accept that, but for now, he would pay a portion of his son's way. Again, my friend insisted on paying his own way.

At the end of the second semester, he flunked out of college.

He was so focused on accomplishing the goal his way that he did not pace himself. He would not slow down long enough to look at the big picture. He did not realize that it was more important to accomplish the goal than to achieve the goal on his terms. Unfortunately, he has never been able to go back to college. Even though he would never admit it, I believe he regrets the decisions he made. I hope his children will allow their father to help them, if he can.

As you can see, the need to rest and pace yourself is just as crucial in accomplishing your goals as it is in driving. You don't want to be the car that ran off the road because you were too stubborn to stop, rest, and reevaluate your situation.

Toll Booths

I am sure you have heard people say, "If I had a nickel for every time that happened, I'd be rich." Well, the city of Chicago has put that saying into operation. If you have ever had the good fortune to travel Rt. 294 around Chicago, you've had the joy of paying a $1.00 toll about every seven or eight miles. If you are driving around the city, there are at least six toll booths where they collect this mobile tax.

If you have never traveled this route and do not prepare for these toll booths, it can be very frustrating. During heavy traffic, the lines get long and slow. If you don't have the correct change, it can slow you down further while you get change. If you are prepared, and you have the proper change, you can toss your money into the bin as you drive through. It counts the money and raises the gate so you can fly through quickly when the traffic is moving. You may also invest in an EZPass, which allows you to drive right through, and the toll is charged to your credit card. It pays to prepare.

With many goals, there are toll booths along the road—points at which you must stop to fund your journey. If you are attending college, you must pay for your books and courses each semester. You must pay your rent monthly and purchase your food on an ongoing basis. If you are financially prepared, or you are earning money on an ongoing basis, then you breeze through the toll booth and hardly slow down. However, if you are not prepared to pay for the next semester, or you have to skip a semester to raise the finances, this toll booth can slow you down or even bring your journey to a halt.

Try to anticipate all the expenses and other resources you will need to accomplish your goals. Add some extra funds to account for the things you did not anticipate. Talk to people who have done what you are going to do, so you will know what hidden costs may arise. Be encouraged as you pay your tolls along the goal road you are traveling. Each time you pay a toll, you are that much closer to the end of the journey.

Mile Markers

Back in the late '70s, there was a growing demand for CB (citizens' band) radios. The general public had found out what had always been the staple of truck-driving communication. Movies like *Smokey and the Bandit* and songs like "Convoy" had the average American putting CB radios in their cars. The airwaves were overloaded with people driving "four-wheelers" trying to talk to truckers and one another. There was a unique language they used, and it certainly made the trip a little more relaxed if you were traveling alone. (I admit it; I had one, too).

One of the frequent questions was, "What's your twenty?" This is CB lingo for "Where are you?" The standard response would be, "I am northbound on Route 23 at mile marker 1-7-2."

On most major highways, the mile markers are small signposts that appear every mile with a number on a green reflective sign. The numbers go up from one border of the state and down from the other border. The average traveler seldom uses them unless the exit numbers correspond to the mile markers (i.e., exit 324 is at mile marker 324).

You can tell when you are getting close to the designated exit by watching the mile-marker signs. The only other time travelers are glad the markers are there is if they have car trouble. They can get help directed to them by letting the tow-truck driver know what mile marker they are near.

If you have ever been to a 10K or a distance race, they have the distances marked in intervals along the route. The mile markers are there to help the runners know how far they have run and how far they must go. The runners use the information to time and pace themselves.

From a goal-setting standpoint, it is nice to have some mile markers along the way to measure your progress.

In the college scenario, each time you finish a semester, you have reached a mile marker. Like they say, "Three down and five to go." Acknowledging the mile marker gives you a sense of accomplishment and pride that you are advancing.

For every goal you set, identify some mile markers along the road.

If you are losing weight, stop and congratulate yourself after you have lost five pounds. Do it again at ten, fifteen, and so on until the goal is complete. If you are building a garage, stop and admire your handiwork when you have finished each phase. Celebrate. Maybe this is going to dinner or having a beer. What you do to celebrate isn't as important as it is that you celebrate in some way.

As you advance toward your goal, the mile markers will come and go with regularity. Before you realize it, you will have completed your goal and will have fond memories of the little victories you had along the way.

Turns and Junctions

GPS technology is impressive. You can find a street in any town. If you ask the app to give you directions from Columbus, Ohio, to Dallas, Texas, it will tell you which roads and highways to use, how far to go on each path, and what direction to turn at each intersection. It is designed to give you as many details as you need to get to your final destination. It assumes that you have never been there and have no idea where you are going. The detailed information provided gives you all the turns ahead of time, and you know which way you are going to turn when you get there.

> If you know the direction you will turn before you arrive, it helps eliminate confusion and misdirection later,

This level of planning is needed in goal setting as well. You need to identify as many turns and junctions as you can ahead of time. If you know the direction you will turn before you arrive, it helps eliminate confusion and misdirection later, and then it becomes a simple adjustment instead of a significant direction change. This helps keep you on track and saves time and frustration.

Any time you have to make a slight adjustment in your goals process, that is equivalent to a *turn*. In contrast, a *junction* is an important decision that needs to be made in the midst of accomplishing the goal.

For example, if you were rebuilding a 1966 Ford Mustang, there could be a variety of turns or junctions in the process. If you needed to patch the front fender, an example of a turn may be the fact that you need to put two coats of finish instead of one.

This issue does not change your general direction; however, it may delay the next step slightly. However, if you must replace a fender, you may have just come to a junction. You now must seek out a source for the fender, and then decide if you can afford it (or your wife will allow you to spend the money).

At this point, you must make a decision which direction you are going. You may have to decide to rebuild that part, even if you planned to buy it. Depending on whether you buy a fender now, take a month to restore it, or take three months to save the money; this junction affects the time it takes to complete this stage of your goal.

If you owned your own home and wanted to build a new house, this would be considered a preeminent goal. I would classify it as mainly a financial goal, but it has many attributes of a life-changing goals as well.

Let's examine many of the junctions and turns you might know about ahead of time.

Once you have decided that you want to build a new home, the real process begins. First, you meet a Realtor or builder to find out how much new housing costs in your area. You must then determine whether you have the resources to build the home of your dreams.

You must determine how much your current house is worth before you can decide how much house you can build. For this, you need to have an appraiser value the property. Once you receive an approximate value of your property, and assuming you can sell it for that amount, you evaluate your financial picture.

Next, you would contact a banker to see what mortgage rates are and roughly how much your monthly payments would be. Then, depending on how it matched up with your income, you would proceed.

If you found that you could afford a $1,000-per-month mortgage and the new house requires a $1500-per-month mortgage, you have to make a decision. Can you afford the extra $500 per month? (If so, you made a *turn*—a slight adjustment.)

If you can't afford the extra money, then you have reached a *junction* (a point at which you must make a new decision). Do you buy less house, do you raise more money, or do you stop the process and continue to live where you are? Your old house may look pretty nice after going through this process.

Let's assume you can afford the house and you proceed. Because you are a goal setter, I am sure you are resourceful enough to get the additional capital somehow. Now you come to a series of adjustments (turns) and some decisions (junctions). Remember, whether it is a turn or a junction is determined by how important the decision is.

First, you must pick out a lot and determine if the cost corresponds to your budget. Next, you must decide which type of house you want—big and roomy with two stories, an attic, and a full basement, or small and cozy with a screened-in porch? Each to his own, but everything is a decision.

Now comes the fun part! Carpet or hardwood floors? Paint or wallpaper? Carpet or tile? And all the other choices along the way. In most cases, each of these is a mild turn along the road to a complete home. You come to a junction only when you run into a problem where a significant decision is required. The builder probably doesn't care whether you want to paint or use wallpaper, but it is important to you, and you must communicate your preference. However, if you want an extra ten feet added to the width of your garage so you can store your boat, decisions must be made. Will the house plan and the lot size support this extra space? How much more will it cost, and how will it look? If you don't like the cost, or if it doesn't fit on the lot correctly, you must decide what to do.

It may be hard to believe, but builders will tell you that home projects have been made and lost over "simple" decisions like this. The more of these turns and junctions you can anticipate in any goal-setting project, the less anxiety and stress you will encounter along the way. As in driving, when you know a junction is coming, you can be watching for the road signs.

If you are not anticipating the turns, it is easy to miss them and find yourself way off the track that you had set for yourself.

Vacation or Business: The Highway or the Scenic Route?

When most people travel, they do so for either a business trip or a vacation. If you are on a business trip, you usually are on a pretty tight schedule and have limited flexibility with your time. If you are on vacation travel, you may or may not have flexibility in the schedule. You must determine at the beginning of your trip, how urgent is your travel?

You may have to arrive in Miami on time to catch a cruise ship. I doubt that you will waste much time, and I am sure you will be at the airport far ahead of your scheduled flight.

However, if you and your family have decided to drive from the Midwest to Maine in the fall, you may want to take your sweet time getting there. There may be places along the way that you want to stop and see. There may be points of interest you find along the way that you did not know about when you left.

If you are not on a tight schedule, you have the flexibility to go sightseeing. At some point, you will want to get on with your trip so you can see Maine, but if you get there at 4:00 p.m. instead of noon, it probably isn't a big problem.

Because this is your life and your goals, it is your choice as to how rapidly you accomplish them. The more important a goal is to you, the faster you will want to achieve it. Often, people have a lifelong desire to achieve a goal, yet their busy lives allow them to work on it only occasionally.

These are the people who have a real interest in accomplishing a goal but are content to accomplish it as time allows. Sometimes you will see people opening their own business after they have retired. They have spent a lifetime learning about something, and now they have the time to make it a full-time focus.

There is no right or wrong decision as to the speed with which you accomplish your goal. Realize, however, that any delay you cause may have long-term effects on when you can move on to the next step. You may take ten years to accomplish a college degree. The longer it takes, the longer it will be before you are qualified for the job you want.

Determine ahead of time whether you are on a business or pleasure trip. If you are on business (accomplishing a life-changing goal), stick to the road and don't go sightseeing. There will be plenty of time for that after you have finished. If this is a pleasure goal, take your time, but don't spend so much time sightseeing along the way that the leaves have all fallen by the time you get to Maine. Remember why you are on this journey in the first place, and don't allow so many side trips and delays that you never reach your destination.

Pit Stops

You have probably seen an auto race on TV. As the driver pulls into the pit box, the crew is waiting and ready. One guy has the jack, and another has the wrench. One guy has the fuel, and others have the tires. As soon as the car gets to the designated spot, the pit crew goes into action. They can refuel, change tires, wash the windshield, and hand the driver a drink—all in about 14.3 seconds.

The announcers often comment about the efficiency of the pit crew. The part that the spectator never sees is the decision-making process on the part of the driver and his team as to when he should stop in the pit.

If the driver stops too soon, he will waste time, and his car won't be able to hold as much fuel. If he stops too late, the car may blow a tire or run out of gas. Maybe you've seen a race either won or lost because the driver skipped the last pit stop and ran out of gas on the last lap. Sometimes the gamble pays off, and sometimes it does not.

> Maybe you've seen a race either won or lost because the driver skipped the last pit stop and ran out of gas on the last lap.

Determining when to stop is based on what the crew knows about the car, fuel consumption, distance, and road conditions. You certainly would not expect the car to make it 500 miles on one set of tires and one tank of gas. It may be a noble try, but the driver is not going to win any races if he reaches beyond the car's capability.

Earlier, we compared the process of achieving a goal with a long trip that requires an overnight stay. You will have to decide approximately how far you will go each day, how often you will stop, why you will stop, and what your destination is each day.

Let's say you decide you will travel approximately eight hours for the day, at 60 miles per hour, going roughly 480 miles. If your gas tank takes you only three-fourths of the way, you realize you will have to stop along the way to get gas. You also assume you will need to make a couple of restroom breaks, and you decide you will take a brief rest and eat your lunch along the way. Then you will stop at suppertime for the day.

It is essential for you to decide what you will accomplish when you stop, to maximize your driving time. For example, you don't have to wait until you're almost out of gas to pull off the road. You can fill up when you stop for lunch.

It doesn't necessarily take a great deal of thought to plan these stops, but it can help your trip go more smoothly and reduce your driving time.

When you are working on a long-term goal, you must plan these pit stops as well. If you don't, you could burn out because you are trying to get all the way to the end without resting and refreshing yourself.

Each of us needs to make brief rest stops on the road of life. It may be a restful weekend or a special evening out. These stops help you take a mental break more than anything. Sometimes these little breaks are just what you need to get through the tough times. You don't have time to take a vacation; just do something that refreshes you enough to stay the course.

Then there are times we need to refuel. We are feeling somewhat weary, but we know we can't stop yet. Many people take time out to meditate, consult with a friend, or listen to a motivational podcast. Whatever you need to do to refuel, take the time and do it.

I had a friend in college who would play basketball before studying for a test. He would exert all his energy on the court, clear his mind, and then hit the books. It seemed somewhat unconventional, but he believed it helped him study.

When you have worked hard toward a goal for a while, sometimes you need to take a break and give yourself a chance to regroup and refocus on what you are trying to accomplish. This break needs to be long enough to refresh, but not so long that you allow yourself to get distracted or lose momentum.

Sometimes, you are fortunate enough to be able to schedule a vacation in the middle of your goal. Semester breaks in college are a good example. These stops allow you to get away, refresh, refocus, and return to school ready to tackle the next semester.

Don't be so aggressively fixated on your goal that you don't take at least a short rest stop. You don't want to burn out, and you sure don't want to miss a chance to refocus. It does take a little time if you stop, but you usually make it up with increased vigor and focus as you start out once again.

> "If I only had an hour to chop down a tree, I would spend the first 45 minutes sharpening my axe."
> —Abraham Lincoln

Check the Map Board

On our holiday trips to see my grandparents, we always stopped at rest areas along the Ohio Turnpike. Like most rest stops, there was usually a large map board of Ohio and the turnpike. There was always a big red arrow pointing to a spot on the map with the most important words: "You Are Here."

As kids, it was always fun to look at the board to see how far we had come and how much farther we had to go. Now, in adulthood, I check that map board to make sure I am on the road I am supposed to be and to make sure I have not missed a turn somewhere. The map is also helpful to determine how much farther we must go before we face a change in direction or the trip ends.

As you work toward accomplishing the goals in your life, don't forget to stop occasionally and check the map board. Review your goals, and refresh them in your mind. Review the goal direction, and make sure you have not gotten sidetracked along the road. If you have, this is the time to realize the error and correct it. If you never check your direction and progress, you may have gotten so wrapped up in your goal that you missed an essential element.

For example, one of the things I have noticed about the computer era is that it is very easy to get wrapped up in what the software will do instead of focusing on what you wanted to do with the software. You start out with a clear mission to accomplish, and suddenly you find yourself trying all these new "tricks" with the software. They are exciting but have absolutely nothing to do with the finished project.

Many a time, we have heard the story of the brilliant young student who heads off to college with the goal and determination to become a lawyer. As he gets into the "college experience" and loses track of his goals, his grades began to slip.

Unless this young man comes to his senses or someone can get his attention, he will find himself at the end of his undergraduate work with a grade point average that is not acceptable to the top law schools. Because this student never stops to check the map board and review his goals and direction, he does not complete his goals because he did not stay the course.

It is beneficial to have advisors or confidants whom you trust, who can speak the truth to you. Review your goals with them periodically. Make sure you are going in the direction you decided in the beginning, and if you are not, figure out what adjustments you need to make. Once you have made these decisions, waste no time putting them into action and getting back on the straight and narrow.

Reviewing your goals is essential to your well-being and your mental health. It keeps the goal at the front of your mind and keeps it crystal clear. It realigns your thinking and your actions and almost ensures that you won't get lost along the road.

People who are not goal-oriented may feel that you are obsessed with your goals. I would contend that you are focused and wise to keep the goal in front of you. If you are obsessed with anything at all, it would be the sincere desire not to get lost along the way and miss the opportunity to succeed. It matters not what others think because once you accomplish the goal, you are way ahead of the pack. Others will remember how dedicated you were to yourself and your cause.

There is something exciting about seeing the "You Are Here" sign. It shows you and the world how far you have gone, and it reminds you how much farther you need to go. It provides a sense of accomplishment and offers excitement for the future.

Food and Fuel: Rest Stops

Regardless of how fast you want to get to your location, your vehicle holds only so much gas, and everyone must use the restroom occasionally. If you are driving through the desert, between Las Vegas, Nevada, and Phoenix, Arizona, there are only a few places to get gas, and they are far apart. Making sure you get gas when it's available can make the difference between arriving safely or sitting in the hot afternoon sun waiting for help to come when your vehicle runs out of gas.

When my kids were young, I always joked that they announced their need to use the restroom just as it disappeared in my rear-view mirror. When you have young kids, they don't always know when they need a potty stop. You have two choices. You can continuously be frustrated, or you can plan your rest stops.

When we make our long trip to Canada every summer, it takes about ten hours of driving. A couple of different times, we didn't pay attention to where we were and passed the towns with restaurants and good rest stops. Tired, hungry children make the trip challenging. Over the years, we have worked out a consistent plan on where and when we stop. We always take time for a sit-down lunch in Buffalo, allowing me (the driver) to rest a while, so we are not trying to do a big meal once we arrive. Knowing our lunch destination gives us a mini-goal and keeps us pressing on.

When you set a goal that spans a good deal of time, such as a year or more, it is worthwhile to plan some breaks or vacations. Break your goal down into smaller pieces. Not only can you achieve one piece at a time, but you feel like you are accomplishing something.

Imagine if high school or college were a four-year commitment with no breaks for summer, spring, or even Christmas. You picked four classes that you took nonstop for four years. It would be a formidable undertaking, and I believe a lot fewer people would attend college. As it is, a four-year college degree is divided up by semesters, and each semester is three to five classes. As you pass each class, and each semester, you work closer to your goal.

Sightseeing

When you take a long trip, sometimes you come across a billboard that directs you to a sightseeing location that is not on your list. Assuming that you will not be passing this way again soon, you might want to realign your schedule for the day and take some time to stop and see the sights. It does not prevent you from getting to your destination, but it may delay the arrival time.

When you stop for sightseeing, let yourself enjoy it. No one wants to see the sights while Dad sits and looks at his watch every five minutes, trying to push the family along. Take your time, enjoy, and create a memory.

When you stop for sightseeing, let yourself enjoy it.

In life, we do not always control our schedule, nor are we able to see very far into the future. When we set goals, there is an assumption that everything will continue at the status quo so you will be able to progress without interference.

However, most goals take some time, and along the way, things can get delayed. Many a student has been on the four-year path to college graduation, only to have an unexpected illness, family death, car accident, or financial issue, delaying the completion of the degree to more than four years. The key is to embrace the delay, do what is needed, and then get back to task.

The delay may not be detrimental. It may be very positive. Maybe the delay is because of the birth of your child or grandchild. I would say that is very positive and worth delaying your goal for a time. Maybe you were planning on a specific dollar amount assigned to your project or purpose, and your daughter came home one weekend and announced she is getting married. Suddenly, there are other demands on those same dollars.

Do not allow the delay to derail the overall goal. Just make sure you get back on track after your "sightseeing."

Limitation: Time

Sometimes we have a great deal of freedom when we are working on goals. Other times, we do not. If you are trying to lose ten pounds before the wedding in two months so you can get into that dress or suit, then you know what your time frame is. If you have a plan to improve the landscape on your property, the project may take years. In this case, there is no deadline.

If you are trying to do a project for work, someone else may be setting your goals and timelines. However, when you are setting goals for yourself, you are making these decisions.

Timelines and deadlines are not your enemies. Setting a specific date to reach a portion of your goal is very important. It helps keep you focused and pushing for the purpose. Imagine that the wedding is over a year away. Do you think you will start losing weight today, or closer to the wedding date? Most people would wait.

Even if you are setting your own goals and there is no finite time requirement, it is always in your best interest to set time goals for yourself. As you will see when we break down the goals, you may have several timelines at different intervals as you progress through the process. I often see people set goals with no timetable or deadline. Years from now, they will still be talking about the goal but will be no closer to accomplishing it.

You may also need to measure the goal against a predetermined timeline. In my profession, it is not unusual for the Securities and Exchange Commission to come out with some new requirements every few years. Your license and ability to continue your practice may now require you to obtain an additional certification or to pass a test. If you want to keep your job, you will complete it by the deadline.

There is one thing I have learned about time—you may not hit your goal at the exact moment you expect to. However, people who set goals usually reach them. Maybe not on time, but much more often than those who do not set goals at all.

Many people throw out ideas of what they will do, such as "I want to retire at sixty-two" or "I want to start a business someday." The people who set a goal and then work at it may not retire until sixty-three, but others get to sixty-five or sixty-six and still can't afford to retire. You may not always hit your goal by your self-imposed deadline. However, you will be more

You will be more likely to reach your goal when you set a time limit. Those with no timetable often never achieve their goals.

likely to reach your goal when you set a time limit. Those with no timetable often never achieve their goals.

Limitation: Resources (Money, People, Job Flexibility)

Every goal requires resources, even if the only resource is time. Determining what resources will be needed is an integral part of the planning and goal-setting process.

To start a business, you need capital, inventory, employees, a business location (even if it is your basement) customers, suppliers, advertising, etc. Lining up those resources is an essential part of the plan.

To lose weight, you need the following: a weight goal, your beginning weight, a bathroom scale (even if you do not like what it says), a diet plan, proper food, the know-how to cook it, a kitchen scale to weigh the portions, a calorie book or app, and a timeline. When your friends find out you are on a diet, they will ask you, "How much have you lost?"

Imagine if you said, "I don't know. I don't weigh myself; I just feel good about what I am doing." Of course you wouldn't say that!" You want to say proudly, "I have lost ten pounds so far!"

Building a home requires capital, coordination with a builder, lumber, a plumber, electrician, etc.—all coordinated and appropriately timed, as needed.

The same goes for determining what resources you need to accomplish your goal. Because it takes resources to reach the goal, it takes time to decide what those resources need to be and to coordinate them for your success.

Limitation: Reality

Sometimes, reality gets in the way of reaching your ultimate goal. If you are determined to lose thirty pounds in six weeks, and you stay the course for twelve and can lose only twenty-five pounds, I call that a success, not a failure. Your body type may not want to cooperate. Take it as a victory. Be proud of what you have accomplished. Whether you believe it or not, you have achieved much, much more than many who never set a goal in the first place.

A few years ago, my neighbor decided he was going to remodel his bathroom. He had done projects like this before and was very talented. He made his plan and did his homework. However, once he tore out the old bathroom, he found some electrical problems that he was not qualified to handle. Instead of taking a chance on electrocuting himself, or burning the house down, he reluctantly (and at his wife's pleading) finally called a professional electrician to do that portion of the job. With that complete, he finished the project himself. Reality got in the way of him doing the project alone, but he still completed the remodel successfully—and safely.

As much as we would like, we do not control everything that surrounds us. Reality can get in the way. Take the win, and do as much as you can. Then hold your head high and move along.

Incidentals and "Accidentals"

Everybody expects expenses with any route they take. You need to buy gas and maybe stop for a meal or two. I refer to these expected expenses as *incidentals*. They are part and parcel of your traveling expenses. No sane person would head on a trip without money in their pocket and some way to pay for each expense on the trip.

However, if you get into a snowstorm and suddenly have to spend the night, this is an "accidental." It was not on your radar and certainly not a planned expense. However, you must be prepared to fund this temporary expense to get to your destination. In the case of severe weather, you can't go home anyway. You might as well be tucked into a safe and warm hotel room and be delayed for a time rather than to try to push through a dangerous storm to save a little money. Besides being in possible danger, the stress of proceeding past this point is not worth it. Adjust your schedule and accept the delay.

With your goals, you may be delayed by a medical situation, family problems, or any number of issues that can slow your progress.

Keep your eye on the target, and get back on the proverbial road as soon as possible.

SET YOURSELF UP FOR SUCCESS

There must have been some reason you picked up this book. Maybe there are some pressing issues in your mind that caused you to take the time to read about setting goals. There must be something you want to change or accomplish that made you want to learn about goal setting.

I am not going to guess what those things are. It is not essential for me to know. It is crucial for *you* to identify what they are and write them down. You must write them down, or they will be just another passing thought or idea—and pass they will.

However, I will venture to guess that whatever issue you are dealing with has passed through your head several times before you got to this stage. That is normal, and it's how most change takes place. The difference between your current issue and many of the other areas you have changed is that you are unsure how to proceed this time. That is why you bought the book.

Let's go down this road together. In this chapter, I share with you some fundamental concepts that can increase your chances for success in reaching your goal.

The Time and Money Question

Now it is time to get ready for a powerful exercise. Get out your device or a pad of paper and take notes as we go. The real benefit of this exercise is that when it is complete, you will have a very clear road map for where you are going and how you are going to get there.

The first question I always ask people is the Time and Money Question: "If time and money were not an issue, what would you like to do?"

Take time now to answer this critical question. You may want to take a day or two to think about it. There is never just one answer. Usually, there are multitudes of things we want to do, be, or change. Write them all down, and be very specific. Don't worry about how ridiculous your ideas may sound or whether you believe you can achieve them. It is your wish list, and only a starting place. Don't worry about putting them in any order right now. Just write them down.

Follow Your Heart

Maybe you knew immediately what you want to accomplish, without too much thought. If that's the case, it's because you have been thinking about these issues for a long time. The goals that come to your mind the fastest generally are the things in your life that cause you the most concern.

Don't be afraid to follow your heart in this exercise. There are no limits. Don't keep it inside you. Let it out, and write it down. It is your sheet of paper, your future, and it is confidential. Now is the time to get all your ideas on paper.

> The goals that come to your mind the fastest generally are the things in your life that cause you the most concern.

Many people have no idea what they want to do or be until they take some time to think about it. That's allowed. There is no hurry here. If you did not know what you wanted to do or be, it is because you have not been thinking about it. The only difference between the people who know what they want and those who do not is *time*.

If you have no idea what you want to do or be, it could be because you have been taking care of others. You may be a parent whose children are grown and on their own. You may be an employee who has been serving in a "go-nowhere" job. Or maybe you have had to set your life aside to care for an ill parent or other loved one.

Plenty of people have succeeded in life after fulfilling other commitments for many years. Susan Boyle was nearly forty-eight when she tried out for TV's *Britain's Got Talent*. She had spent a good part of her life up to that point caring for her mother. She became an overnight, world-renowned star at the age of forty-eight. It was not too late for her.

It's *never* too late!

> "The time for action is now. It's never too late to do something."
> —Antoine de Saint-Exupery

Start by Addressing Frustrations

If you are unsure of what you want to accomplish, then I suggest that you start with a small goal. The first goal you set in your life doesn't have to be to climb Mt. Everest. Maybe organizing your desk or office is a starter goal that helps you get going.

Sometimes, the best way to begin setting goals is to figure out what frustrates you the most. (Now, if it is your mother-in-law, good luck!) Most of us have areas that continually frustrate us. By identifying those, you can begin to determine what you want to change.

Here are some examples of potential frustrations, along with solutions:

1. You are frustrated that your clothes do not fit well. *Write out a plan to lose weight and/or work out.*
2. You can't find anything on your desk at work, and this causes delays and frustration. *Take time to identify that as a problem, and begin the process to fix it.*
3. Every time you pull into the driveway, you see the paint peeling at the top of the house under the eve's trough. *Make a plan to paint it, or begin the process of getting a quote from a professional to get it done. At least you will be moving forward.*

Years ago, when I started my business, a business coach showed me an easy way to identify and eliminate frustrations. He said, "Write down everything that drives you crazy or frustrates you in your day-to-day work." I wrote each problem on a separate sheet of paper. Then he asked me what I thought the solutions would be for each issue, and I wrote them down.

Then we identified if I needed to learn specific skills to rectify each problem and how long we thought it would take. Finally, we prioritized the pages in the order I wanted to get things done. Some were short-term fixes (goals), and others took longer. But at the end of a few months, I was able to rectify most of the issues that had been creating havoc in my day-to-day life. This is a simple but powerful lesson in goal setting.

Sometimes, the little things cause the most frustration. Fix those first, just to make the day better and give you peace of mind.

Many of us are so busy living our lives that we never spend any time thinking about how we want to change things. Some of that

> Many of us are so busy living our lives that we never spend any time thinking about how we want to change things.

comes from being knee-deep in reality, and some of it comes from our backgrounds.

I have a friend who regularly came to me with ideas for businesses or other ways to make a living. He was a laborer and had a wife and five children. He knew he needed to change and was always looking for an idea. When I asked him the Time and Money Question, his response was, "I don't know. I've never had the time to think about it." He was so busy trying to provide for his family, he had never taken the time to focus on how to make things better.

Many people accept that life is what it is and figure that is *all* it is. They take what life gives them and try to be happy about it. Have you ever felt this way? In your past, you may have been discouraged from "daydreaming" about what you could be someday. Many parents discourage their children from trying something new because there is a risk that they may fail. If they fail, they will feel bad, and Mom and Dad don't want their kids to feel bad.

The only problem with this attitude is that it does not allow any room for individual achievement and choice. Even though the safe route is meant to protect us and keep us "safe," it leaves everything to chance and in the control of others. It also does not allow for the fact that we are responsible for our own lives and for the choices we must make as adults. Where would our modern-day transportation be if the Wright Brothers quit after their first attempt at flight?

First Instincts Are the Best

Sometimes, we get philosophical in our approach to change. We sit back and dream of walking the sands of a beautiful beach and think, "Someday that will be me!" But then we go back to doing the same old stuff the same old way.

Other times, we think we have to accomplish Great and Mighty Deeds. Remember, every invention starts with someone's dissatisfaction with the status quo. Changing your life is sometimes a result of no longer being satisfied with how things are and making a point to improve them.

As you begin the process of changing your life, work on the things you can impact first and fastest. When you think about changes you need to make, again, your first instincts are those that are probably causing you the most frustration. Start with those. This results in immediate change and a feeling of accomplishment.

As you progress, then increase the scope and difficulty of your goals. If one of your goals is to walk in the sands of a beautiful beach, then find out how much a four- or seven-day cruise is, and begin to save for it. You don't have to be rich to enjoy a goal like that—just smart and patient.

You Must *Decide* to Succeed

America has long been at the forefront of discovery, invention, and growth that have been an example to the rest of the world. From the day the pilgrims set sail for the New Land, America has been a place where people can come to make a new life. It remains so today for many people from troubled countries. There is an opportunity awaiting those who can make it happen.

What is it about this country that makes its people so determined to succeed? Why can anybody from China, Vietnam, Iraq, South Africa, or Latin America come to this country and start a business of their own? There are several answers to this question, but I would contend that one of the key reasons is that people in America can and do decide to make their lives better.

People who wanted a different life started the New World, and that has fostered an attitude toward blazing new trails ever since. In the early days, people literally blazed new trails to the West, followed by the railroad and the pursuit of gold. In more modern times, the United States has blazed trails in space flight, computerization, and cures for many types of medical maladies. We are a people who not only accept growth and change, but a people who *expect* it. Even our model of government demonstrates and supports the ability of any person to choose his or her lifestyle and profession.

But then it gets complicated for the average person. Having the freedom to choose how to live life is one thing; having the knowledge and courage to make it happen is quite another. Depending on the type of household you came from, you may have felt that you had very few choices—or you may have felt like the world was your oyster.

In the United States, you can go to college if you have the grades and the resources. If you did not have either, you might have felt like you were robbed of the chance to go to college. However, we always hear about young people who came out of poverty, worked their way through school, and beat the odds. We also hear about young people who were born with "silver spoons in their mouths" who squandered away a Harvard education.

There are a variety of reasons why this happens, but I believe the main reason is that, at some point along the way, these people decided to let their lives happen instead of making things happen.

A *decision* is key to everything that we do. You can go to high school, get good grades, and have the money to attend college, but unless you make a conscious decision to go in that direction, it will not come to pass.

Unless you make a conscious decision to go in that direction, it will not come to pass.

Imagine, if you will, that you are standing on one side of a door, and I am standing on the other, and we cannot see each other. If you have a desire to come into the room, there are two ways you can enter. You can either open the door yourself and walk in, or you can knock on the door or call me on the other side of the door, and I can let you in. In either case, you would need to *decide* you want to come through the door, and then you must take action. The issue is not *how* you get through the door. The point is that you *decide* to come through.

It sounds so simple, but it is a concept that many people have never been able to grasp with regard to their lives. Very seldom is life going to sweep you off your feet and take you exactly where you want to go. The main reason most people do not accomplish the things in life that they wish for is that they have never made the conscious decision to go after them. They sit on the sidelines, waiting for life to decide for them. Then it seems that the decisions that "life" made for them are rather mundane and allow them to waste away on the sidelines. Even worse, many lost souls seem to die off because they have no purpose or focus in their lives.

Anywhere you go, you meet people who have accomplished great things or have beaten the odds and mastered a difficult skill. There is always that question as to why they were able to reach that level when many others, with greater or equal talent, could not. Typically, the difference is the conscious decision to pursue that success.

You must decide to succeed. If you do not choose to achieve, then you are essentially agreeing to fail. If you can't go that far, then can you see that you agree not to succeed. (Same thing, in my mind).

For example, you decide to get in shape by getting off the couch and going for a run. Choosing to sit on the couch and not go for a run is a decision *not* to get into shape.

I heard a story one time that I would like to share with you. A boat is sailing on the ocean. The boat contains an elephant, a tiger, a parrot, and one person, and the boat runs aground on an uninhabited tropical island. Assuming that none of the passengers are hurt, what will each of the beings do once they land on the island? The parrot will probably fly around, look for food, and end up perched on a limb in a tree. The elephant may walk around looking for food and water, take a swim in the ocean, and eventually come to rest on the beach somewhere. The tiger will do much the same, and for this story, we will assume the tiger does not eat the elephant or the man for dinner.

The man, however, will almost immediately begin improving his environment and his situation. He may build a fire for warmth and light. He will most likely try to find a source of water and create some shelter for himself. He may even use the elephant to move trees or reach high branches. If the man is stuck there for a long time, he will probably form tools and spears out of rocks and branches. He may decide to carve a canoe out of a large tree trunk and try to sail back to civilization.

Man's ability to evaluate the situation, think, and then improve his fate is what separates him from the other beings on the island.

The man could just sit on the beach like the animals and hope that someone, somewhere, might come along and save him.

However, man's ability to evaluate the situation, think, and then improve his fate is what separates him from the other beings on the island.

Even though each of us has the God-given ability to change our environment, many of us do not feel like we can. The world is full of people who are blaming their present situation on something that happened to them when they were growing up. They use this as a crutch, and it keeps them from stepping out and taking charge of their lives.

Obviously, real situations affect us for our entire lives. The difference between those who do and those who do not is one single word: decision. Science has proven over and over that many behaviors, even though they are not hereditary, are repeated down through the generations.

Studies show that children of alcoholics are prone to alcoholism. Adults who were abused as children often turn out to be abusive parents. However, these behaviors are not hereditary traits. If it is a behavior, then it had to be learned. If it can be learned, it can be stopped or altered, and new traits can be developed.

The first step in making any change in your life is admitting that there is an area that needs improvement. Because it is difficult for most of us to be objective people about our own behavior, we must count on family and friends who love us. We need to be willing to ask the hard question ("What can I do to improve my situation?") and then listen to the hard answer and take action.

If you happen to be married, you know what I mean. Your spouse sees all those habits in you that you choose not to see. When my wife is about to bring one of these subjects up, she will say something like, "I have a question" or, "I want to bring something to your attention." Even though this makes me cringe a little, she usually brings up an issue that does need to be addressed. As uncomfortable as it may seem, it is much better for a friend or loved one to approach you with a problem than it is for your boss to have to bring it up—or for you to continue on a path that's not ideal for you.

Once the issue is on the table, you are free to decide to change or improve in that area. You are also free to choose not to change the situation, but there is something very awkward about ignoring a fault that is brought to your attention. Now you are not only ignoring the mistake, but you are arrogant about it as well. Sooner or later, the issue is going to come back around, and you will have to deal with it.

A decision is the match that starts a fire. It is the key that starts the ignition. It is the force that moves you toward a goal, and it is a point of no return. You can stand and look at the wood pile for hours and hours, but it will not burn until you decide to light the flame. From that point on, the pile of wood and kindling are changed forever.

The decision to light the fire sets all other things in motion, and from this point on, nothing will ever be the same. Yet before you decide to light the fire, you have some decisions to make.

> A decision is the match that starts a fire.

How big of a fire do you want? Do you keep it burning by adding more wood, or do you let it die out and start again? Regardless of the decision you make, things will never be exactly the same as they were before you lit the match.

Life is very much the same as that stack of logs and kindling. Maybe you have put several things in order in your life, so you are prepared to go in a specific direction. Perhaps you have gone to college and are now thinking of going to law school. Maybe you have been dating the same person for two years or thinking about buying a house in five years. You may have been checking out law schools, looking at engagement rings, or saving money for a down payment on a home. All this is great, but it is of absolutely no consequence until you decide to move forward.

From that point on, everything will be different. Your decision to go to law school leads to applying and choosing a school, studying, getting good grades, graduating, and finding that first job in a law firm. Your decision to buy a house leads you to a Realtor and a banker, a mortgage, and finally taking up residence in your new home. Your decision to get married leads to wedding plans and honeymoon plans and continues throughout your life, including children, grandchildren, and in-laws. From here on out, you will be forever changed because you decided to act.

As you can see, making a decision leads to countless changes and can come with enormous responsibility. For this reason, many people are afraid to make that vital decision because they are afraid of where it will lead them, or they do not have the confidence to see it through. This is somewhat understandable, but I must remind you that doing nothing also comes with consequences and responsibility.

If you chose not to buy a house, then you choose to continue to pay rent. If you continue to pay rent, then you build no equity in a home, etc. If you decided not to get engaged, then you may be choosing to stay single or eventually discontinue the relationship. It is up to you. It is important to realize that every decision to accomplish a goal brings change, and every decision *not* to change brings consequences as well.

Regardless of what areas of your life you want to improve, there will come a time when you will need to make the specific decision that gets the ball rolling. Don't be afraid of it. Embrace it as an essential step in your self-improvement.

"It is in your moments of decision
that your destiny is shaped."
—Tony Robbins

Journaling Adds Another Layer of Resolve

Thinking about your situations and solutions is certainly a step forward, but writing them down can be an even more powerful exercise. Consider documenting your decisions and then journaling about all the details that accompany them.

Journaling is a powerful way to keep track of your life. You can write down your trials, tribulations, victories, and innermost feelings. The real advantage is that it gets your thoughts out of your brain and onto the paper. Now you can own your decisions and begin to work on solutions instead of having it all roll around in your head. Writing these important thoughts and decisions down adds another layer of resolve to your journey of self-improvement.

When you document your journey toward change in writing, it can be very satisfying to go back to the beginning and see all the great things that have come to pass because you were willing to decide to improve your life and situation. It is quite amazing to review and see what you have been able to accomplish over the years.

My wife and I have both journaled over our three decades of marriage. We have established two rules:

Rule #1: My journal is private—I can share it with you, but no peeking on your own.

Rule #2: No limits—you can write as you feel! Sad, glad, elated, pissed—write it all down, and get it out.

If you are a believer, journaling can be a powerful part of your devotion time and an opportunity to clearly see God's hand in your life. It is fascinating when you go back and look at the changes you have made and see how you walked through them over the years.

> "Writing is another powerful way to sharpen the mental saw. Keeping a journal of our thoughts, experiences, insights, and learnings promotes mental clarity, exactness, and context."
> —Stephen Covey

There Is No *"Try"*!

Many years ago, I met a young man who was a friend of a friend. A financial advisory firm had just hired him. When I asked him about the job, he told me he was going to "try" that for a while. When he left that day, I told my wife, "This guy is not going to succeed at his new job."

She asked me why.

I said, "He has not *decided* to succeed. Before he even started, he was saying, 'I will 'try' this for a while.'"

The unspoken sentence is "If I do not succeed, then I will try something else."

We must make up our minds and decide that we are going to succeed. We must do everything in our power to make each effort a success. If our hearts and minds are not committed to the process, then we are not willing to hang in there when things get tough. We must *decide* to succeed, not *think* we might succeed. It seems like a minor difference, but it changes everything.

For the record, the young man I just mentioned lasted less than four months at the new job. You should have heard his list of excuses to explain why the situation wasn't a good fit. The truth is, he didn't decide ahead of time that he was going to succeed.

Excuses Are the Reason for Failure

Excuses get us nowhere. Maybe I decide to go for a run, but I will run later. When is later? If it is this afternoon, then it's likely to happen. If it happens five years from now, you are probably not going to get into shape.

People are not usually specific about their goals. They set a goal but then are ambiguous about when they will start the process, or when they want to complete the objective. It's easy to make excuses when the goal is vague.

With weight loss, there is always a holiday or vacation or party coming up that causes people to delay the start of their program. I can't start before Thanksgiving, then Christmas, then New Year, then Uncle John's birthday party, then vacation, then Fourth of July, then Labor Day, and right back to Thanksgiving. In the meantime, they put on another ten pounds.

Break Your Goal into Subgoals

How many goals should you pursue at once? The best answer I can give you is, "It depends." Remember, every large goal is made up of several small goals.

To get your nursing degree, you must complete the four-year program, which means you must complete each year with good enough grades to pass the class, which means you must study and go to class, which means you must read the material and notes, meaning you must manage your time and sleep well. To accomplish a significant goal like this, you will have enough subgoals to keep you busy.

If you choose to be physically fit, you must work out so many times per week, eat healthy meals to manage your weight, and get proper sleep.

Or, if you are trying to improve your opportunities at work, your goals and subgoals might look like this:

1. Read specific books on relationships and leadership. Then list the books in the order you will read them—one, two, three.
2. Become skilled at public speaking. Sign up for a Toastmasters public-speaking program.
3. Improve your listening skills. Listen to recordings, podcasts, and/or TED Talks, and practice the techniques and conversations with your friends and family. (Don't tell them you are practicing.)

It is very common to have one primary goal, two to three secondary goals, and then subgoals for each of these.

I encourage you to review the different types of goals in chapter 4—family, mental, social, physical, etc. It is not uncommon for people to have a list of goals under each category. You certainly can't work on all your goals at once. However, many of your goals in different areas of your life will overlap.

You have family goals to provide a certain level of lifestyle for your family, or you want to pay for college for your kids. This requires you to manage your financial goals from your early years of marriage. Can you advance some of your career goals so you can make the income needed to send your kids to college? All are important goals and have many overlapping aspects.

> **Many of your goals in different areas of your life will overlap.**

It is also possible that goals can change over time. You may have a list of work-related and career goals. They might overlap as you accomplish goals on the job you hopefully set yourself up for advancement.

Suddenly, you get the promotion you have been working so hard for. If that means you continue to work in the location you have been, then you now have a new set of job goals based on the new responsibilities. Give yourself time to adjust to the new job, and then start looking to the future again, setting new goals for advancement.

Maybe your promotion causes you to move your family to a new city. Now you have other questions to answer. "Do we move to a bigger house this time or buy something more modest? Does the move allow me to step up in my social goals, live in a higher-end neighborhood, send our children to a private school, or get a membership at the country club?" Maybe not, but the move brings all these goal questions to play at once.

What you choose and where you decide to live often depends on where you are in your life, your climb, and your income. My advice is to take your time on these many decisions that come at once. For example, maybe you step up in house size but choose public schools initially. You can always make the transition to private schools in the coming years, if that is important to you.

Don't jump too far, too fast. You don't want to have to go backward. I have seen many a family take a new opportunity with increased income. Before they barely start at the new job, they have committed every extra dollar, plus some they didn't plan on. You are better off to take it in steps. It's better to have an above-average income in an ordinary house than to have an above-average house with an income that is barely able to cover the bills. Overextending yourself can limit your freedom.

REPLACE BAD HABITS WITH GOOD

The couple with three kids looks at each other. They are living in an apartment with two bedrooms, and there is no room for the kids to play, no basement, and no peace for Mom and Dad. They have talked about buying a house but have never done anything about it.

They decide to see a mortgage agent at their bank. They find out that they have decent credit, but they would need about a 10 percent down payment on a house. On a $200,000 home, that would be $20,000. The couple has little in savings, so they are kind of stuck. However, the process gets them thinking. They are motivated to commit to saving money because their living arrangement is not getting any better.

One day, they get serious. They send the kids to the grandparents' home for the day and sit down and take a serious look at their finances. They itemize their expenses, line by line. They look at their income and outgo, and then they started making some hard decisions.

They reason, "We can cut back on the cable bill and maybe bundle some of the services. That cuts out $100 per month. The car will be paid off soon, so that frees up $250 per month. We were going to get a new car, but we really need a new house, so the car will have to last." They scrimp and scrape and make some new decisions. Eventually, they figure they must cut about $400 per month out of the budget. They will apply every dime of that money to the down payment.

Besides, the dad occasionally gets some overtime. In the past, they just let it land in their checking account, and it disappeared over time. They had pizza delivered here, went out for dinner there; here a buck, there a buck—everywhere a buck-buck. The money dissipates. Not anymore! All overtime gets immediately funneled into savings. They figure it will take at least two years to build up the down payment, but they are determined.

Suddenly, everything they do filters through their desire to buy a house. Mom and Dad go without birthday and Christmas gifts for each other. They speak to their family and let them know that they will be tightening the belt for a year or two. They are not antisocial, but they will be having picnics in the backyard instead of spending the day at the amusement park. It is only for a season, but it will be worth it.

In eighteen months, they have the down payment. In addition, their credit score has miraculously improved because they have more savings and less debt. With the down payment in hand, they go back to the bank, get approved, and begin the process of finding a house.

It is incredible what people can do if they want a goal badly enough and are willing to make the changes necessary to achieve it.

This family needed several things to accomplish this goal:

1. Dissatisfaction with their current situation
2. An understanding of the process and what was required (down payment)
3. Feeling that the goal was important enough to them to cause a change in their spending and saving habits
4. Willingness to pay the short-term price to reap a long-term benefit
5. Sharing their goal with the important people around them

It is quite interesting when you go back and speak to people years later. They can tell you, in detail, the process they went through to get their house, for example. Better yet, they continue many of the good financial habits that helped them get the house. Those changes have become good habits, and they often continue to save and approach other expenses in the same manner.

> "You'll never change your life until you change something you do daily. The secret of your success is found in your daily routine."
> —John C. Maxwell

Chain Makers and Chain Breakers

Changing ourselves for the better sometimes requires that we discontinue bad habits and/or adopt good habits.

In every family situation, there are chain makers and chain breakers. A *chain maker* is the continuation of some behavior or activity common to your family. A *chain breaker* is the discontinuation of such an activity. The chains can be bad or good.

In my own life, here's an example of a chain maker. My grandfather took his family fishing at a specific lake in Ontario every year. My father took his family to the same lake for family vacations, and I continue to take my family. I have missed only one summer in twenty-eight years of marriage and don't plan to miss out again. I hope my kids continue the chain.

However, a chain maker also can be a bad habit carried on through the family. It may be drinking or some other bad behavior. Many child abusers come from abusive situations. Sometimes, people continue with a bad habit or behavior because that is what they were taught, and that is what they know—for example,. "Dad yelled at me, and now I yell at my kids. That is what I know."

Being a *chain breaker* means you discontinue a habit or behavior that you had growing up. These chains are hard to break. To break a family chain, the first thing you must do is to recognize that the activity is detrimental and harmful to yourself and others. This essentially means that you have been doing something wrong for all these years. It may say that your parents and family did something wrong, too. This can be difficult to admit. Don't look for support from your family, especially if they continue in the activity.

> Being a chain breaker means you discontinue a habit or behavior that you had growing up.

Once you identify that your actions must change, now you need to change and act differently. You may not know precisely how to behave, so breaking the chain is tough. It may take time to adjust to a new habit or lifestyle. You must decide to change and then learn positive activities to reverse the momentum of the negative activities. You may have to set this as a longer-term goal, as it may take some time to adjust.

The real goal is to take the best from your family experiences and sift out the bad. Maybe your dad was an alcoholic, but you had memorable family vacations. Continue the vacations, but control the alcohol use, or eliminate it. Or maybe your parents were good savers and money managers, but then they made their kids feel guilty for every expense incurred. Take on the good money habits, and change the personal management habits. I know—it's easier said than done.

Here is an example of one man's attempt to break the chain of a familiar family habit.

Ron came from a big family. They often got together for picnics, birthdays, and cookouts. The men who gathered always consumed a good deal of beer. As the evening went on, the jokes got louder, as did the laughter. The kids were encouraged to help.

"Bring Uncle Joe another beer," someone would say. There was never any trouble, but the wives frequently drove home at the end of the evening. Summer, winter, Christmas, and Easter, this was the pattern of Ron's family.

When Ron got married, he and his wife went to all the family events. Ron sat with the men, and the tradition continued. Ron's wife came from a different background. She didn't object to the drinking, but she did object to the volume consumed and the money spent. Her main objection was the example that the men set for the children. She and Ron discussed it often, but nothing changed.

A couple of years later, Ron Jr. was born. Without a word being spoken, everything changed. Suddenly, Ron saw the world through different eyes. He determined that he wanted to set a good example for his son.

Ron and his wife still went to family functions. However, Ron began to introduce other activities to help people do things besides sit and drink. Summer picnics now included volleyball and horseshoes. Indoor birthday parties and Christmas gatherings brought card games and board games. Nobody in Ron's family ever realized that he had helped break the chain for himself and others.

Maybe your mom worked full-time, and you want to be a stay-at-home mom. Or maybe your mom stayed at home, and you want to be a career person. Either way, you are deciding to break a family chain. Maybe your dad was loud and abrasive, and you choose to be more relaxed. Or maybe your dad was easygoing, and you feel you need to be tougher. Whichever way you lean, buffer the result so you are not at one extreme or the other.

The broad sense of righting a family wrong can drive people for decades and can be hidden deep down inside. As parents, we like to emulate the things that worked in our family as we grew up.

Because we want to change the things that didn't work, we may overcompensate.

Interestingly, our adult children may even reverse some of the behaviors we worked so hard to break. And life goes on!

Crisis Often Brings Focus and Priority

People are stubborn. Why is it that a doctor can get you to do something you hate, but you could never get yourself to do it at all?

How many people do you know who stopped smoking after they had a heart attack or stroke? Those same people now walk in the mall every morning, but before, they would never get out of their easy chair to go for a walk or get a little exercise. They now eat kale, bran, and broiled fish, whereas in the past, it was salads with bacon and blue cheese dressing, pancakes, and fried fish (with hush puppies). It is regrettable that we often have to be "forced" to change our ways only after we have taken lousy care of ourselves over the years.

"If I had known I would live this long,
I would have taken better care of myself."
—Unknown

Even if a crisis is the only thing that could get you to change your ways, at least you have the opportunity to change the future. When you stop smoking, you add years to your life. When you improve your eating habits, your health and energy can improve. When you start saving money, it is incredible what you can accomplish in a few years. If crisis got you to this point, and you are still standing, then make the most of it, and order broccoli next time instead of French fries.

To add some urgency to your pursuit of goals, you could create a crisis if you are not in one already. Create a pressing issue or reason to make a change. Have you ever been around people who are going to be in a wedding in five months or are going on a cruise? They can suddenly be highly motivated to lose weight if they are going to be wearing a bridal gown or a swimsuit.

However, with enough focus, determination, and planning, you can set and achieve goals without having a crisis to motivate you.

Decide that you no longer want to wait for the crisis to come before you make a change. Decide that you would rather have a long talk with yourself instead of waiting for the doctor to have that talk with you. This way, you are deciding on the changes without having to recover from a real crisis. Make it a big deal, and do not stray from the plan.

"In a time of crisis, we all have the potential to morph up to a new level and do things we never thought possible."
—Stuart Wilde

Routines and Choices

When trying to determine which goals are important and what needs to change, it is a good idea to review your routines and choices. Much of life is a continuous string of routines and choices. Many times, we do not stop to think about which they are or what we need to change to facilitate *getting there*.

Routines

Routines are not a bad thing. They help us organize our day, our work, and our lives. We rise at a specific time, shower, get ready for work, get the kids up, and get them off to school. We begin our day with our home routine. We arrive at our work, get our coffee, check our email, and start the process of our work routine. We create policies and procedures at work so that the company runs smoothly, and then we get adopted into other systems, such as when the IRS wants your taxes paid.

We drive to and from work on the same path every day, at approximately the same time because we have figured out when the most opportune time is to get home with traffic. What we don't realize is that we are driving next to thousands of other people whose routine happens to line up with ours, at that same time.

Then we get home and start the home routine again. We have dinner, make sure the kids do their homework, get their baths, and get them to bed. Then you have your evening routine. Maybe you get a cup of tea, settle down with a book, and relax for an hour or so before you head off to bed, all set to begin the routine again tomorrow, in much the same way. Routines add structure and direction to our daily lives, without having to recreate the wheel every single day. However, if you have teenagers, you may feel like you are starting at square one every day.

There is absolutely nothing wrong with routines as long as they have a positive function in your life. But let's change the above routine slightly.

You finish work at five and head out the door, like any other day. Today, you decide to stop at a local watering hole and have a couple of cocktails with some friends. You stay longer than expected and get home after the kids are off to bed.

There is certainly nothing wrong with this scenario, assuming you communicated with your spouse or family. However, what if this visit to the pub becomes part of the routine? Now you are spending time and money that you should spend on your family. You come home late most evenings and are not back in time to have dinner with your kids or spouse. Now you start getting home rather late and are having a tough time getting up for work the next day. You are exhausted from work, and it begins to affect your performance.

Is it still a routine? Yes. But the habit has now become destructive. It is a regular pattern of activity, but it has now disrupted your life.

Choices

Whether you realize it or not, somewhere along the way, you decided to change the routine. You chose to go to the pub one evening, and then you chose to begin repeating that choice, making it part of your routine.

Assuming you are not an alcoholic and can, in fact, control your decisions going forward, how would you change the situation?

First, you would need to identify that the routine you are on is not yielding the results you desire. You must be honest with yourself. However, in this scenario, I am quite sure that your significant other has already been "honest" with you about the situation.

> You must be honest with yourself.

You would need to evaluate your pattern and routine and determine that to be a successful parent, you need to be home most evenings with your family. At this point, you must choose to change your routine to not include the stop at the pub. Depending on how entrenched you are in this situation, you may have drinking friends who call you crazy and try to encourage you to drink with them. Making the right choice in this situation is essential.

Let me provide a different example that may not be so obvious.

Bill and Sandy have a good home, good jobs, and a healthy home life with three kids. They are active in their church, school activities, and the kids' sports. They run from one event to the other, and as a couple, have decided to support their kids in any way possible.

One of the things that is happening is that the credit-card bill seems to be mounting slowly. They always paid it off in full every month, but recently, they have seen the balance climb. They cannot identify any substantial expenses that have occurred. However, the bills seem to grow regularly.

When they start to review the monthly expenses, they begin to see a pattern. There are many fast-food and pizza charges on the card. Because the family is so busy, they find it hard to eat at home each evening, so they are frequently eating on the run. Weekends have ball tournaments, so they eat out again and again. They tell themselves they are supporting their kids and that nothing can be done, but the problem continues to mount.

Even though this has been their routine, Bill and Sandy are now aware of the problem and have a desire to rectify it. Now it is time to make some choices and change the routine. It is not always easy.

Because Dad must go straight from work to ball practice, he takes an extra sandwich with him when he leaves in the morning. Maybe Mom has a sandwich lunch packed for the family on those evenings when they would usually run through the fast-food lane. Perhaps the family takes breakfast food and sandwich fixings with them for the weekend tournament so they do not have to eat out so often.

It may not be as much fun as eating out; however, these changes still get the kids fed and bring the finances under control. Bill and Sandy choose to alter the routine to the total benefit of the family, not just for the sake of convenience. Nobody forces them to do this; they choose because it is in the best interest of all.

Review your priorities. If one of your goals is creating problems in some area, figure out how to solve the problem while still achieving the goal. Or alter the goal.

As you can see, setting and achieving goals requires constant review and adjustment.

SIX OBSTACLES TO OVERCOME

If goal setting is such a powerful exercise, why doesn't everyone do it? Some of the obstacles originate within us, while others relate to the way other people react to our efforts to improve. Let's look at some common obstacles that prevent people from setting and/or achieving goals.

1. Lack of Awareness

The first and most common reason people don't set goals is that no one has ever taught them about goals.

In my family, one of the many things we like to do for recreation is to fish. We go to great distances and effort to fish. My grandfather loved to fish. He taught his son (my father), my father taught his children, and now we are teaching our children. However, because my grandfather did not hunt, my father did not learn to hunt, and he did not show me. So I have no intention of taking up hunting or teaching my children.

The point is, most people do not know how to set goals because their parents did not know how to set goals. It's the same principle. In this day and age, because schools do not teach goal setting, there are only two ways you can learn: either someone else teaches you, or you learn through a book like this, an app, a podcast, a blog, or some other platform. I was fortunate enough to have someone show me how to set goals, as I mentioned earlier.

2. Fear

Another main reason people do not set goals is they are afraid of failure. You may have heard the phrase, "Nothing ventured, nothing gained," but I think most people subscribe to the phrase, "Nothing ventured, nothing lost" (especially dignity and self-worth). It is much easier *not* to try something and not fail than it is to attempt something and fail. No one can make fun of you if you never put yourself in a place where they might laugh at you.

It may seem easier now to pass on an "opportunity" to fail, but in the long run, it is much more difficult when you look back and see that you passed on those same "opportunities" to succeed.

In my mind, there are two kinds of fear: the fear of failing and the fear of missing out and not making the best of a given opportunity. Many are afraid of the first. If you can learn to be fearful of missing the opportunity, it can indeed drive you.

I have seen authors refer to fear as the acronym for "False Evidence Appearing Real." It suggests that many of the fears we have may not be genuine problems but are created in our minds. Our ability to see past the fear and envision ourselves succeeding is crucial to our success.

Are we more afraid of people making fun of us or of being stuck in go-nowhere jobs for the rest of our lives? Are we more fearful of struggling financially or struggling to be better? Are we more interested in what others think of us or what we think of ourselves? My experience is that we are often more worried about what others think about us. The truth is, they are not concerned about you; they have their own concerns and problems. Focus on your own journey!

Focus on your own journey!

"I'm not afraid of storms, for I'm learning how to sail my ship."
—Louisa May Alcott

3. A Low Self-Image

Earlier, I mentioned the positive impact vision can have on people and their goals and dreams. There is no doubt that this can be true. However, people who have challenges with their self-image may find a vision to be self-defeating. They may see themselves failing and picturing the shame that comes with that failure.

Sometimes, this is because people cannot overcome the pain they've experienced or the mistakes they've made. Their past causes them to be reluctant to try things; they do not want to fail again and feel that pain. Therefore, they stop stepping out and attempting things, often making excuses along the way. They say things like, "That's not for me" or "That will never work."

They see others stepping out and succeeding, but they just don't have the confidence in themselves and are not willing to take a risk. Maybe they are worried about the financial risk or the possibility that they will look foolish. Perhaps they can't face themselves or others if they don't succeed. Whatever their reason, they find fault with the opportunity and then never try.

I remember a coworker years ago. He was very talented, well liked, and well respected. He had repeatedly proven that he could deliver results. Yet because of the culture at the firm, he was never going to be in leadership. He was a reliable number two man. Also, his wife was always nervous about him being out of work. She was only interested in him "having a good job," not pursuing his dreams or goals.

Because that culture was not conducive to growth, I chose to leave and pursue a new career. He and I talked in general about that at different times. It always seemed to me like he could achieve more, but he always said he didn't think he could ever make the break.

The day they announced that I was leaving, he stepped up to congratulate me. However, I could sense that he was thinking, "I wish I could make the break and do something different." He never left that company, and he got passed around from department to department. Unfortunately, he passed at the young age of forty-seven. I always felt he died without fulfilling his destiny.

Because his wife put a great deal of pressure on him to have a good job and not rock the boat, coupled with his lack of confidence to take any risk at all, he settled for a position that never really tapped his ability to lead, grow, and see what he was capable of in the outside world.

Don't let that happen to you! Set your sights on your best possible future, and then set goals and take the actions necessary to succeed.

4. Lack of Support

A fourth reason people do not set goals is that they do not have enough moral support from friends and family to get the encouragement they need along the way.

Let's use a sports team as an example. While the offense is trying to reach its goal, the opposing defense is trying to prevent the offense from scoring the goal.

Similarly, in life, at least two defenses will arise. The first is the self-doubt that may remain in you from other "attempts" at making changes to your life. The second may be the well-meaning "help" of friends who try to discourage you from setting goals or chasing your dreams. They may tell you that setting goals is fine, but you will just cause yourself disappointment when you fail. I have some strong advice if you have friends like this: get different friends, at least while you go through this process.

People may try to discourage you for many reasons. Some may feel like they are helping you and saving you from pain and discouragement. Others may not have the same vision you have and see the task as impossible. Others may not want you to succeed because your success will leave them behind, magnifying the fact that they are unwilling to change. It sounds cold, but it is not uncommon, especially in a work environment.

Surround yourself with positive, supporting people who will encourage you and root for you. Be careful who you share your dreams with; you may pose a threat to them.

> **Be careful who you share your dreams with; you may pose a threat to them.**

College football teams recruit high school seniors from all over the USA. Pro football drafts the best of last year's college teams to help ensure they have the strength, the strategy, and the power to overcome the opposition. If the football teams of the nation can recruit others to help them win games, wouldn't it be appropriate for you to enlist all the help you need to reach your goals?

Books and tapes, mentors and friends, bosses and parents can all help by encouraging you to reach your goals. Surround yourself with people who will root for you to win and help you get back on track when you fall behind. This support can be crucial in the hard times and when you get weary.

Some people are already somewhat successful but do not realize that adding goals, direction, and discipline to their habits can take them to higher levels of success than they ever imagined and to succeed more quickly. Until someone teaches you, or you have the desire to learn the process, you will never realize what you can accomplish with goals in your life.

5. Criticism and Fault Finding

Maybe you come from a family that regularly puts you down. Perhaps you have a work environment where you are told you will never succeed. Maybe you come from a bad relationship that causes you to question your ability to get along and nurture others.

Being on the receiving end of criticism and fault finding can be difficult to overcome, and it won't change quickly. However, if you begin to believe that all that was said about you was not true, then you start to act and show that you are different from what was said.

There is no doubt that parents, teachers, coaches, other adults, and influential people can have a positive or negative impact on your life. If those influences are positive, they can encourage you to reach great heights.

However, if those influencers are negative, this can have a significant impact on your future, and more importantly, what you *believe* you can accomplish in the future. Regardless of how you feel about yourself initially, the constant negative input from an influencer can change your vision of your future—and even change your core belief about yourself and your abilities.

A parent or influencer who continually finds fault with all you do can make it hard to believe in yourself. When they add phrases such as, "You will never amount to anything," it can confirm and reinforce any self-doubt a person may have. Now, in addition to the difficult task of succeeding in a complicated world, you must also overcome the negative concepts that are embedded in your psyche.

Sometimes, the most challenging thing you must do is separate yourself from the negative influence of others. This may require that you move away from those who love you, or minimize contact. Sometimes, the only way to build your self-worth is to get away from those who consistently find fault and tell you that you will never succeed. As you can imagine, this can be a difficult choice.

People have different reasons for finding fault with those around them. Some are just mean-spirited. Others are jealous; they don't want you to succeed because they fear it might draw attention to their own issues. Still others are just critical in nature.

Again, many times, fault finding is well-intended. Maybe the parent or influencer has had failures of their own in the past, and they do not want you to experience the same pain they did. Therefore, they discourage you from stepping out and trying things. They see it not as "Nothing ventured, nothing gained" but rather as "Nothing ventured, nothing pained." If you don't step out and try, then you can't possibly fail. If you don't fail, then you don't feel the pain. It is twisted logic based on bad experiences they've had in their lives.

The truth is, we can't please everyone all the time. Focus on your goals, and tune out the naysayers.

> "There is only one way to avoid criticism:
> do nothing, say nothing, and be nothing."
> —Aristotle

6. Rejection

People lose their jobs for a wide variety of reasons. Many times, it has nothing to do with them or their performance. However, it is common for people to take a job termination very personally. At times, this type of rejection can cause people to doubt their ability. If they begin to believe it was their fault, it often makes it difficult for them to acclimate to a new work environment.

I had an employee who caused a great deal of strife in the workplace. Even though we tried to work with her, we had to terminate her employment. When we finally fired her, she said, "I knew it was only a matter of time." Even though we gave her plenty of chances, her self-image told her she would be fired. She then acted in a manner that caused this to happen. It was a self-fulfilling prophecy for her.

This can often be true with intimate relationships as well. A rejection from a mate can be devastating and cause self-doubt. Then it is harder for people to proceed into the next relationship. They have a poor self-image and now almost expect any new partner to reject them.

Post Visual Reminders of Your Goals Where You Can See Them

As you set goals, it is vital that you see yourself succeeding. Picture yourself in the big office, behind the big desk. Picture yourself vacationing on a beach somewhere, or running your own business. Picture yourself in that size 6 dress or tapered suit after you have lost weight. If you cannot envision yourself succeeding, then indeed, nobody else will.

> As you set goals, it is vital that you see yourself succeeding.

Many people who teach on goals like to encourage people to find visual images of the target and post them in their homes and offices. For example, you might post a slim, trim model of a person of the same sex on the door of the freezer. Every time you look at the picture, it reminds you of the vision of your goal. Does it replace ice cream? No, but it can help you have the strength to move closer to the goal and skip the ice cream.

Find a picture of a beautiful beach, or get a brochure from the resort where you want to go. Post it in your bedroom, carry a copy in your wallet, or make it your screen saver on your computer or phone. Every day, you are reminded of your goal, and that makes it easier for you to make the decisions that get you closer to it.

Maybe you put the picture of a Lamborghini up where you can see it. Maybe you don't really want one, but it represents the lifestyle you would like to have someday. Put up a picture of the boat you want, the cottage you desire, or the lake you want to retire to. Make a mockup of a sign for the business you want to launch, and post it by your goals. You will be amazed at how it plays with your mind and keeps the ideas dancing in your head.

> I am a big believer in making a vision board for the same reason—because it keeps your goals in front of you in a visual way, which is powerful positive reinforcement.

I am a big believer in making a *vision board* for the same reason—because it keeps your goals in front of you in a visual way, which is powerful positive reinforcement. Get a piece of poster board from an art-supply store. Cut out pictures of successful people, nice cars and homes, and other visual depictions of your goals from catalogs and magazines, or print them from websites. Affix these images to the poster board to help you focus on *who* and *what* you want to be.

Many people try doing this in their heads. It doesn't work. There are too many other thoughts interfering. The poster is a constant reminder of the following:

- How you want to look: clothes, shoes, hairstyle, physique
- Where you want to live: sunshine, mountains, beach
- How you want to live: Types of cars, styles of houses
- How you want to be successful: business owner—not an employee

You must believe in yourself. You cannot continually perform in a manner that is different from the way you see yourself. You must begin seeing yourself succeed, excelling, and being accepted. You must start to see that you can make a difference. You must believe in yourself. You may be the only one who does, but at least there is one reasonable person in the room who does!

No one else will be as passionate and dedicated to this idea as you. Keep your goals fresh and visible in your life so they will motivate you to work toward them.

Now that you've learned some strategies for overcoming obstacles, let's examine the "reverse pyramid"—a method of goal setting in which you work backward, breaking a goal down into manageable steps.

THE REVERSE PYRAMID (WORKING BACKWARD)

One of the many challenges of setting goals is identifying the first steps you need to take. It is so hard to look down the road a year or more and know what steps you need to make today as you focus on *getting there*—where you want to be.

Besides, many goals can seem to be very overwhelming when you look at them in their entirety. The old adage "How do you eat an elephant? One bite at a time" really applies to goal setting. It is important to break down each goal into almost ridiculously small tasks that you can accomplish quickly.

Here are two examples from my past.

I was not an accomplished athlete, but I did play football in high school. I can remember the two-a-days[8] in my freshman year. All I could see was two weeks of hell. I was so overwhelmed and intimidated from looking at the big picture that I did not want to start. The next year, I approached it one day at a time, and it was much more comfortable.

Many years later, I had to pass an exam to get my securities license. The books and tapes came in a big box—the book was four inches thick, and there were twelve tapes. After I opened the box, it sat for almost two weeks because of the overwhelming perception of the task at hand. Eventually, I began reading the book one page at a time. Finally, I worked my way through the material.

The "reverse pyramid" is an effective strategy for breaking down a goal into manageable steps.

---

8. Intense football practices in the dog days of August, before school starts—generally two full workouts each day, six days a week, for two weeks.

You look at where you want to be and what you want to accomplish, and you work backward. This way, you touch on most of the essential areas and determine what must be completed first. You start with the final accomplishment and work back through all the steps you need to get to that point. As you go backward, your tasks become more detailed. Let me give you some examples.

Your Life Is a Trip!

Using the trip analogy, let's use the reverse pyramid to plan a trip backward. Let's say you live in Ohio and are driving to Texas. The trip is approximately 1,200 miles, depending on what part of Texas you are traveling to. Obviously, it is farther to south Texas than to north Texas. Because this is a long trip, there are several steps to the planning:

Step 1: Pinpoint where you are going and where you are currently.

Step 2: Determine how far you must travel (total miles).

Step 3: Divide the total mileage by 60 to get an average number of travel hours. We assume an average speed of 60 miles per hour.

Step 4: Determine how many hours you want to travel each day. This determines how many days you will travel.

Step 5: Because you are traveling more than one day, determine the city where you want to stay each night, based on the number of miles you drive each day.

Step 6: Find out which hotels are in the areas where you are going to spend the night, and make your reservation. Availability and cost may alter your travel distance.

Step 7: Make sure your vehicle is ready for travel. You may need an oil change, new tires, or just a fill-up. A lack of essential preparation can cause severe delays on the trip.

Step 8:   Determine how much the trip will cost you. Consider gas, meals, hotel, sightseeing, and some spending money. Then get the money in cash so you can avoid using credit cards. If the money is not readily available, you may have to postpone your trip until you have the funds.

Step 9:   Set a time and place to leave.

Step 10:   Pack and prepare for the trip. If you are taking snack food, or need special clothing for the destination, accumulate these items. Again, if you do not have all the required elements, this may delay your trip.

Step 11:   Get a good night's sleep, and make sure you set the alarm.

Step 12:   Leave. Have a great trip!

Don't Forget to Write!

It makes total sense that you would not start out on a trip of this size without appropriate planning. It is doubtful that you would be sitting around in the evening watching TV and suddenly jump up and say, "Let's drive to Texas right now." People would think you were crazy, and your family would not be prepared to make this kind of trip without some notice.

If you would not make a trip without planning each step, why on Earth would you live your life that way? The planning is worthwhile and can prevent many problems. In thinking through each step, you are bound to prevent many of the potential problems. It does not guarantee that you won't have a flat tire (unexpected expense), but in general, you have a much better chance of arriving safe and on time if you plan.

Now go back and read the list backward, from Step 12 to Step 1. Can you see how ridiculous it would be if you didn't plan the previous step? Many things would be forgotten or difficult without following the steps in order.

Let's use a more common goal. Maybe you have the goal of losing twenty pounds before you and your spouse go on that long-awaited cruise or tropical vacation in five months. Man or woman, you want to look decent in a swimsuit.

Goal: Lose Twenty Pounds in Five Months

Step 1:   Determine your current weight.

Step 2:   Decide what you want to accomplish (you've already determined you want to lose 20 pounds).

Step 3:   Divide the total weight by 5 months. You will need to lose 4 pounds per month.

Step 4:   Divide the monthly weight by 4 weeks = 1 pound per week.

Step 5:   Divide the weekly rate by the number of days—1 pound = 16 ounces divided by 7 days is a touch more than 2 ounces per day.

Step 6:   Determine how many calories you need to consume per day to lose 2 ounces per day.

Step 7:   Make your meal plan, and determine what kinds of foods you are going to eat to hit your daily calories.

Step 8:   Make your shopping list, and go to the store.

Step 9:	Set a starting time and place.
Step 10:	Pack your lunch, and plan your meals each day based on your calorie allotment.
Step 11:	Get someone to encourage you, or better yet, get a team-mate who has a similar goal.
Step 12:	Buy a new swimsuit once you have lost the weight.

As you can see, each step gets more and more detailed. The initial stages are very general, but subsequent steps are very specific.

What Is Your Timeline?

Once you have worked your way down the pyramid, you will have an idea of how long it will take you to accomplish the chosen goal. Sometimes your boss or a situation will set the time frame for you. On most personal-development goals, you set the timeline.

When you set a time goal, an interesting thing happens. Even though you might not hit the time goal, you will probably be way ahead of people who set no goals at all, or no deadline.

I find that often, people who set a goal to have their house paid off by the time they're fifty-five may not accomplish it until they are fifty-seven or fifty-eight. However, they are still way ahead of those who had no goal and won't have their house paid off well into their retirement.

Work with a Mentor or Coach (We All Need the "Police"!)

With the knowledge you have now gained about the desired goal, do you still want to pursue it? It may turn out that you still want to accomplish the goal, but you have to adjust your timeline. Maybe you thought you could save enough money for your goal in three months, but you figured out it will take you five months. Now you need to decide if you can wait the five months or you want to scrap the goal.

Because you know the steps, cost, and timetable, you can determine if you're going to follow through. The decision is up to you. If you decide to proceed, then be determined to finish.

Earlier, we discussed the importance of sharing your goals with a mentor who will encourage you and coach you along the way. I have found this very helpful, especially when I was learning to set goals.

It is essential to find someone who wants you to succeed, has your best interest at heart, and has the knowledge to guide you. It is vital that your mentor is willing to be honest with you, both positively and negatively, and it is vital that you trust him or her.

> It is vital that your mentor is willing to be honest with you, both positively and negatively, and it is vital that you trust him or her.

In a way, your mentor is like the police—keeping you on the right path, safely.

If you have such a person in mind, it is wise to include this mentor in the planning, or at least allow him or her to review the plan before you finalize it. You might be so close to the project that you will not see holes and potential problems. Additionally, if your coach is familiar with your goals, he or she may know something you may not. This may prevent a glitch in the system that may throw you way off track.

One of the challenges of goal setting is that not everyone is as excited about your goals as you. If you are the number 15 salesperson and you want to make the top 10, there are at least five people who won't be excited about your goal.

Also, your spouse is a necessary support, but spouses are not always the best gauge of daily activity. It will be all fine and good until your goals interfere with the family plans.

Find a mentor who will let you share your goals, your challenges, and your struggles and is willing to listen and help you.

Sometimes, a boss can be a mentor or coach—if that person is self-confident and willing to invest in your success. If your boss is worried about you taking his or her job, find another mentor.

I have a friend whom I have known for years. We mentor and challenge each other to grow and improve. We are very encouraging and brutally honest with each other. If you could hear our lunch conversations, it sounds like I brag about my accomplishments, and then she does the same. However, we know each other's goals, strengths, and weaknesses and can help each other. Even though she now lives way out West, I know I can call her and get a clear, honest perspective.

Using our trip analogy, imagine how fast you would drive if you knew there were no police on patrol. Some of us would drive 90 miles per hour. Having that police presence helps us maintain safe speeds for ourselves and others. Coaches can do the same for us. They can tell us when we are moving too fast and need to slow down to get better results. They may also encourage us to pick up the pace to reach our goal.

"A mentor is someone who sees more talent and ability within you than you see in yourself and helps bring it out of you."
—Bob Proctor

What Is the Speed Limit?

We covered the importance of the timeline in goal setting earlier. One obstacle many people encounter when setting goals is being able to follow the anticipated timeline. Even if they are clear about the goal and the process, they may come across obstacles that alter the time frame. Don't worry if this happens to you. Again, you will still be way ahead of those who don't set goals at all, even if you reach your goal later than you anticipated.

We can compare your time frame for completing a goal to the speed limit you have to follow on a road trip. How well you follow the speed limit will determine the time it takes you to get there.

For example, if you determined you can save enough money for three months to buy a car, and it takes you four, this does not prevent you from hitting the goal. Be prepared for some delays on the goal road, just as you are on the highway.

> **Be prepared for some delays on the goal road, just as you are on the highway.**

A classic example of this is college students getting to their final semester of school and needing a class that is not being offered. It does not prevent them from accomplishing the goal; they just achieve the goal one semester later than desired. Let's look at this example in more detail, in terms of the time frame, as well as two other examples.

Example 1: Going to (Back to) College

Let's assume you graduated from high school and you have been in the workforce for three or four years. You have determined that you want to go back to college, but you're confused about where to start. Let's start at the end and go backward. Let's say you are going to graduate from college with a degree in business.

Based on what you know, this will take you approximately four years to accomplish. You may be able to do it in three years if you go during the summers. Based on what you can find out from talking to friends, you will be required to take eight semesters of school, with each semester consisting of fifteen to eighteen credit hours until you graduate.

Check with the college you want to attend, and they will tell you how many hours of classes you will need to complete. (Most colleges have guidance counselors to help new students figure out the required courses.) With this information, you have a pretty good idea of what your education will consist of.

Once you know how many hours you will be taking, you will need to identify the costs. At this point, you may want to go to the bursar's office to find out exactly how much this journey will cost you per semester or credit hour. Once you determine the cost, you can start planning how you are going to pay for it.

The administration office will tell you what you need to do to apply to the college. Someone there will have you fill out an application, submit your grades from high school, and report your SAT and ACT scores. That person might also give you necessary tests in math and English to determine at which level you will be placed in these classes.

Fulfilling any one of these steps may require additional time and effort. For example, if you have not taken the SAT or ACT test, you will need to find out when they are offered and schedule a time to take the tests. Don't get discouraged! The beginning steps are required to get you going in the right direction. This is precisely why you go through this exercise—to identify all these steps so you know what you are dealing with and how long it will take you.

Also, they may steer you to the financial aid office if you may be eligible for loans or grants. It will take a little time to handle all this, but it can be financially worthwhile.

Once you have determined and identified all these details, you will be able to calculate how soon you can start back to school, based on time requirements and your financial situation. Once this is determined, you can begin working toward going back to school.

Realize the importance of starting with the final outcome—going back to college to get a degree—and then working backward through a myriad of details to get to where you are now. Now you have a road map of what you need to do and where you need to go. Take the first step, and head down the road. Because you have taken the time to build the reverse pyramid, you now know what steps to take in sequence.

Once you take step 1, you can then take action to complete step 2. Then go to step 3. You have a reasonably clear plan for your future. As you accomplish each of these subgoals, you are slowly but surely moving toward your final goal. Congratulations! Before you started, you didn't have any idea where to go or how to get there. Now you have a clear path.

You can use this system with any goal you are pursuing. It takes some time to build the reverse pyramid, but I hope you can see the benefit. Trying to decide where to go today, without working your way backward through the plan, is quite a gamble. You may or may not head in the right direction. If this happens, it is easy to get discouraged, and then you may never accomplish the real goals in your life.

> Trying to decide where to go today, without working your way backward through the plan, is quite a gamble.

If you haven't noticed by now, the scenario I often use when exploring a goal is the issue of going back to college. This is not by accident. Of all the people I have helped accomplish their goals, the one area I constantly come across is the person who wants or needs to go back to school but has no idea where to start.

People who do not know where to start often are afraid to start at all. It can keep them frozen in a frustrated state of inaction, even when they know what they want to do. If going back to school is not in your future, please don't disregard the concept. It works with any goal that has multiple steps.

Example 2: Getting Out of Debt

Getting out of debt is another common goal I've helped many people achieve.

Let's assume you have $6,000 in credit-card debt; you are paying interest on it every month. You set a goal to get out of debt. You are currently making the minimum payment of $135 per month on your credit card(s). At this rate, you are not paying the debt down very fast, and you are probably charging more each month than you are paying down. Let's work backward on the reverse pyramid.

Goal: To be entirely out of credit-card debt

You may want to get your banker or an accountant friend to help you with the number crunching. You need to develop an amortization table, which will show you how much interest and principal you are paying each month. It can also show you the effect of adding additional amounts to your payment each month and how long it will take you to pay off the debt.

You look at your statement, and it says the balance is $6,000. You determine that, by paying only the minimum payment, without putting another dime toward the card, it will take you five years to pay the debt off. (Assume a percentage rate of 21 percent and that you pay the minimum payment of $135 each month).

You determine that if you add $50 per month to your payment, you can pay the balance off in three years. Now decide what you have to do to scrape together an extra $50 per month. Maybe you choose not to buy coffee at work, and you take your own, or you choose to pack your lunch instead of eating out. Maybe, just maybe, you decide you can live without cable TV for the duration and apply that amount toward the balance. However you choose to save the money, you must be diligent in applying it toward the debt each month.

Once you are satisfied with the payment amount and the time frame to pay off the debt, you must eliminate that expense in your life.

Then you have to do two more things. First, you must stop using your credit card—don't buy something unless you have the money to pay for the item. Second, figure out a way to set the needed money aside each month in a place where it will not get spent. Now start paying off the debt. When you have it paid off, you can go back to having cable TV, or you can apply the extra toward your car payment or mortgage. Good luck!

As you work backward on the pyramid, two main things happen. First, you identify each of the essential steps needed to accomplish your goal. And second, it helps you determine the time frame that will be required to achieve the goal.

Example 3: Saving for a Home, Retirement, or a Child's College Education

Saving for a major expense over time is another common goal people have.

In this case, take almost the same steps as in example 2. The difference is that you are keeping the extra money in savings each month instead of spending it.

Determine how much money you will need to save to accomplish your goal. Try to determine how much time you have to achieve this goal. If you are fifty-five and you want to retire at sixty-five, you have ten years to save. The amount of time you have will determine how much you need to save each year to accomplish the goal. Again, you may want to get an accountant or financial advisor to help you with the math. They are familiar with the process.

Once the amount is set and the time frame is determined, then you must decide how you are going to squeeze that money out of your monthly budget. Again, define what you are *not* going to spend so you can save the dollars. The other thing you must decide is where you will put the money you are saving. You don't want the cash lying around; you can gain some interest if you put it in the bank and some growth if you invest it in stocks or bonds.

Now that you understand the process of goal setting, whether forward or backward, let's look at how you can benefit from setting a five-year plan for yourself.

CREATE FIVE-YEAR, AND LONGER, PLANS

Most people think goal setting is something you do one time. You set a goal to lose weight, hit it, and then move on. For most people who have genuinely embraced goal setting, however, this couldn't be further from the truth.

My experience while working with trainees and mentees over the years is this. They generally set one or two goals because they are required to accomplish some job-related goal, usually to achieve a certain amount in sales or to keep a job. They reluctantly embrace the process out of pure survival.

Sometimes, people finally decide to lose weight or go back to school, and they are very determined to achieve a goal in that specific area. They set no other goals except for that one. They are often surprised to find out that the process is not only successful but somewhat addictive (in a very positive way). Once you understand the goal-setting process, then it permeates every area of your life. As we discussed, you may have personal goals, work goals, family goals, etc.

When you see the power that goal setting provides to you and your future, it is easy to get hooked. Going through those times when you seem unfocused or have no clear direction, you quickly realize you have gotten away from your plan. You go back to your list of goals, review, and get back on track.

Once you have gone through the process of setting goals for each area of your life, it does not take long to realize that it will take more than a year to achieve many of the goals. Many goals build on top of one another. This is very evident in education. You can't get the master's degree without the bachelor's degree, and you can't get the PhD without the master's.

You and your spouse may have a goal to be debt-free. This can take several years to accomplish. If you have a list of credit cards to eliminate, then you pay off the first, then the second, etc. Because there is only so much extra money you can put toward this process, you must allow yourself time to knock the debt down.

Now that you have decided to be debt-free, that requires that you stop building up debt using the credit cards. Ouch! This means you must manage your monthly expenses more tightly so you are not relying on the credit cards as a buffer. It may also dictate that you curb your travel, vacations, eating out, and other spending. This seems painful, but you can achieve it if you decide to make these changes together. When you choose to stay at home and eat burgers and mac and cheese, it tastes a little better when you realize you didn't spend $50 for that evening's dinner. You are working toward your goals together.

I find a five-year plan to be ideal.

If you look ahead and see that your credit-card debt will be paid in two years, then what is the next step? Is it to begin to save for a down payment on a house, your children's education, or your retirement? Once the credit cards are paid, immediately reassign those dollars to another goal.

With this example, you can see the benefit of the longer-range plan. I find a five-year plan to be ideal. We can accomplish a great deal in five years by simply setting goals and working to achieve them.

The Benefits of a Five-Year Plan (and Subsequent Plans)

As you work on your goals, they will have different timelines for completion. Some will take a week or a month. Others may take years, such as getting a four-year degree. Others may be ongoing for most of your life.

As you set your long-term goals, it is beneficial to break them down into yearly goals, and maybe even smaller increments. The value of breaking a goal down into smaller increments is the fact that it keeps the goal in focus every day. Without these smaller goals, it would be very easy to lose sight of the end goal.

What if you said, "By the end of five years, I want to be able to retire and move to Florida," and then you just go back to work? You never check your current status or how much you have saved, nor do you begin saving. The chances of you reaching your goal is pretty slim. Sadly, you may never achieve it.

Your chances of success will be much better if you evaluate what your financial situation is currently and begin to research what your costs would be in Florida. You and your partner might decide you should start saving an additional $500 per month toward your retirement goal. Then each year, you revisit the goals and check your accounts and numbers.

Maybe the market was good, and you can reach your goal sooner than you thought. Maybe real estate prices in Florida are down, and you may buy a property at a better price than you expected. Or perhaps the economy is bad, and your savings don't grow as expected. By evaluating your status each year, you can congratulate yourself on what you have saved and achieved and then make any adjustments for the future.

Doing this each year gets you closer and closer to achieving your goal. The truth is, you may need to work six years instead of five to do what you want. However, you will still be retired in the place and fashion that you planned. Most people who don't prepare may eventually retire, but probably not in the same style or with the same satisfaction as those who plan.

As I have stated before, it doesn't take long to realize that a year is not a very long time. To make real changes in our lives, we often need more than a few weeks or months. It is OK to set a goal to lose weight before you go sit on the beach in three months, but if you truly want to change your lifestyle, eating habits, and overall health, it is going to be an ongoing, long-term project.

> Most people who don't prepare may eventually retire, but probably not in the same style or with the same satisfaction as those who plan.

As smart as we are, we cannot always see the future. We think we know how things are going to work out. We make plans based on our expectation of the future. However, we all know that things don't always turn out the way we want—and even if they do, they often change.

Set a five-year plan, and review it every six months or so. Adjust the plan as needed. We do not have to go down the road for five years and *then* discover we made a significant wrong turn three years ago. It is your future, and you want to manage it as carefully as possible. This requires checking in on your progress regularly.

Business/Sales Goals

Many times in business, an increase from year to year depends on the accumulation of new customers, clients, and repeat business. Getting to a certain threshold may be very possible, but it typically takes time. Setting the five-year goal is a good start, but then you need to set yearly goals as well.

Let's say you are a salesperson, and your quota is $1,000,000 in gross sales for your territory. You receive a commission based on hitting your quota, and then a bonus on additional amounts also. If you want to double the revenue in your territory, it would probably be challenging to take it from $1 million to $2 million in just twelve months. However, if your goal for year 1 is $1.2 million, year 2 is $1.4 million, etc., until you reach the 2 million-dollar mark, not only would you be able to celebrate the accomplishment of each goal each year, but you would get to enjoy the bonus you achieved by exceeding your sales requirements.

Also, you will make any adjustments needed each year to get to that final goal. Even if it takes you six years instead of five, you would have doubled your sales in a relatively short time and dramatically increased your income. That should make the family happy. Congrats!

You might be thinking, "It shouldn't all be about money!" Agreed, but many different things motivate people. Maybe working to achieve a sales award or a performance award at work is your goal. Perhaps you want to learn a particular set of skills over an extended period.

I know a man who finally achieved his Master Gardener status at the age of fifty-eight. As long as I have known him, that was one of his goals. It was a hobby for him, so it often took a back seat to kids, work, and family, but he continued to work on his goal diligently, over the years.

He had loads of books and magazines on the subject. He took classes and went to seminars and workshops. He qualified for one certification after another, until he finally achieved his dream. Over the years, he had one of the best-looking yards in the neighborhood, always planting unique flowers and shrubs. It was a treat to go by his place in the summer, as new colors appeared frequently. He was very proud of his work and moved toward his goal for most of his adult life.

Personal Goals

Maybe you are not in sales or do not manage a business. Perhaps you are a stay-at-home parent or hardworking employee of a larger company. Maybe you wonder how goal setting can help you.

So, for this part of the discussion, let's not talk about work goals or financial goals. Let us break down some other areas that are more relevant to your situation.

Your Home

How would you like to improve your home? Can you make it more valuable, more attractive, or more useful for your family? Decide which areas of your home need to be improved. Determine which of these improvements you can do yourself, those that will require the help of a friend, and those that will require a professional.

Rank the home improvements based on importance and your ability to pay for them. Can you complete smaller projects over a weekend?

Larger projects may take more time, and maybe some financing. (There we go with the money again.) Once you have your list prioritized, then set some deadlines for when you want to accomplish each step. This list may keep you busy for a few years.

Your Family

What is essential to your family that they don't have now, or that could improve? If your goal is to provide them with better nutrition, then you will focus on how to provide the most nutritious meals for the best value. Maybe you decide to put a garden in your backyard and grow some of your own food. Perhaps you purchase only certain kinds of meat and vegetables. Perhaps you choose to pack lunches for your family, but you don't want to use processed meats. So you cook the turkey yourself and then slice it and freeze it for the benefit of your family.

Do you have them take vitamin supplements? Which are the best supplements to buy, and why? You may need to do some research so you are confident in what you provide.

What kind of laundry soap do you use? What brand of bath soap and shampoo? This is important to many people. I have a friend who has very sensitive skin, and subsequently, so do her children. She has to be careful about the products she buys. These issues are significant to her because of the challenges the sensitivity has caused her through her life.

Service

What are you passionate about? What areas, charities, or organizations do you think can use your help? Do you want to help build a house for Habitat for Humanity? Do you want to go on a mission trip through your church? Maybe you can't go but wish to sponsor others to go. Determine how you want to make a difference, and then focus your time, talent, and treasure in that direction. Set a goal to sponsor one person on the church mission trip every year. Set up a scholarship at the local high school or private school in your name or the name of someone special.

I have friends who lost their twelve-year-old daughter. Her passion was science, so they sponsor a scholarship each year at the school she. It is important to them.

It's OK to Keep Your Goals Private

You do not need to share all your goals. Some people find that by sharing their goals with other people, it helps keep them accountable. That gives them an extra level of motivation to achieve the goal. But you might not want to share goals of a more personal nature, and that is fine.

Do you have a personality trait you want to change? Are you shy and want to begin to be more outgoing? You can set goals for yourself to work on this. Maybe you go to a wedding, and your personal goal is to walk up to at least three people you do not know and start a conversation. This can be difficult for a shy person.

> You might not want to share goals of a more personal nature, and that is fine.

Maybe you decide to become a better listener. After studying the process, you make a point to engage people and use some of the skills you've learned. You can't really ask the person you are talking to how you did, though. You must learn to discern people's reactions based on how you treat them.

Our Goal to Establish a Family by Adopting

My wife, Shelley, and I got married when we were thirty-three, the first (and only) marriage for both of us. A late start for most couples, but that is life. We tried to start a family after a few years of marriage, with no luck.

After a year of doctor's visits and some nasty fertility testing and medications, we discovered that we were unable to conceive. This news was quite devastating for a young couple who genuinely wanted a family. It took some time to recover from this news, but eventually, we began to explore our options.

We had some friends who were foster parents. They loved the kids they cared for, but the foster-parenting requirements could be daunting. The system required the kids and separated parent(s) to visit each other on a regular basis. Unfortunately, the separated parent(s) have issues, which is why they are separated. Our friends were on a constant merry-go-round of taking the kids to visit the parent, then adjusting the kid after separation, then taking the child back to the parent the next week, and on and on. The primary goal of the foster program is to reunite the children and parents.

We took a few classes for foster parenting and decided it was not for us. Some people are equipped to deal with it all. We wanted our children in our house. We did not want to return them at some point.

So we began to look into adopting.

> Our goal was to have a family by adopting a baby.

You may find this hard to believe, but there are companies out there that make big bucks from adoptions. Some of our friends adopted international children, many from China. More than 160,000 Chinese children, mostly girls but also some boys, have been adopted into families all over the world since China officially opened its doors to international adoption in 1992.[9]

Our goal was to have a family by adopting a baby. Like any goal, there is a process. We had to learn what the process was and how to go about it. I will keep the details to a minimum, but trust me when I tell you, the description is much shorter and less frustrating than the process.

First, you must go through a home study. The state of Pennsylvania (at that time) would send out a social worker to analyze your suitability to be a parent. You had to fill out forms, have blood tests, and get an FBI background check (for real). They interviewed family, friends, and your pastor, and they drilled

9. "Who We Are," China's Children International, https://chinaschildreninternational.org/who-we-are.

down into your finances to make sure you were emotionally and financially viable. This process can take months.

Then there is the process of finding the right adoption. I remember getting a letter from an organization in Colorado. For $25,000, they would make sure we got a baby in about six months. In 1990, $25,000 was a great deal of money, especially for a young couple. The international adoptions were costing around $10,000. At that time, Catholic adoption services took about six months to complete an adoption, but Catholic families got preference. We were not Catholic. Because of the environment in Philadelphia at that time, the state of Pennsylvania adoption could place a black child in six weeks, or a non-black child in one to two years.

We settled on an organization in Pennsylvania, not too far from our hometown. It was a crisis pregnancy center that helped young girls place their babies for adoption. Besides being faith-based, and reasonably priced, they used a different process. The adopting couple completed a profile of themselves: family background, faith beliefs, and education. Also, the organization wanted to know, what are your plans for your child? Do you plan for him or her to go to college? Do you have children already, or do you plan to adopt more than one over time? Some of the girls wanted their babies to be the first or only child in a family so they would receive a lot of attention. Others wanted their children raised in a faith-based home or to be part of a big family, as maybe they had been.

The process of creating the profile took a great deal of time. Some of the exercises and questions stirred up a great deal of emotion. My wife had lost her dad when she was eleven, and this process stirred some deep feelings in her. We had to get letters of recommendation and testimonials from friends and our pastor. We also had to submit pictures of our home, our desires for the child's college education, photos from our vacations, and an outline of the life that we would provide for the child. Like any other worthwhile goal, we worked through each step.

The unique thing about the adoption center we used was that we were not waiting in line for children. Through the state, if you are couple number 25, then you receive the twenty-fifth child. Through the agency we chose, the mother had the opportunity to review profiles from many families and then select the family she wanted for her baby.

It was Mother's Day weekend in May 1994. Shelley and I had gone away for the weekend to discuss our future without children. We had submitted our profile almost a year prior and figured we might not be chosen because we were older than most couples (we were thirty-eight at the time). It was hard for us to be in church on Mother's Day weekend because our hearts ached for a child. We did not want to hinder other people's joy, so we left for the weekend.

I worked my territory that Monday, and then there was a special church service that Monday evening. When we got to church, our pastor hunted us down and told us that the adoption agency had been trying to reach us all weekend. (Before cell phones, remember?) He gave me the number of the agency director, so we went to the church office to return the call.

As I spoke to the director, she asked me the most amazing question. I moved the phone closer to my wife and asked the director to repeat the question.

She said, "We have a little girl who needs a home. Are you ready to be parents?"

Through tears of joy, my wife answered yes! As the director congratulated us, she explained that we would meet the birth mother the next day and get the baby right then. On May 10th, 1994, we met our daughter, Ericca, for the first time. She was three weeks old, weighed 6 pounds and 10 ounces, and had a full head of dark hair.

After we set our goal to have a family, we made the life-changing decision to adopt, and then we did much planning and took many actions to accomplish our goal. Our lives have never been the same since.

We immediately took Ericca to introduce her to our best friends. One evening, there was another special meeting at church. For the first time, I had the great pleasure of introducing Ericca Nicole Hollister to the congregation that had so fervently supported us and prayed for us.

Three years later, we set a new goal and started the process again. By this time, we had moved to Ohio, so we faced an entirely new home study and new rules. We had to find a new agency in Ohio. We had put our name in with a local attorney who handled adoptions through the local crisis pregnancy center and community hospital. Again, we went through the process, checking off one item and process at a time. Within six months, we completed the home study and began the process of waiting—again. During this time, Ericca would often talk about being a big sister. She wanted a little brother or sister so she could be the big sissy.

On Thursday morning, March 25, 1999, I had just opened a folder on my desk to work on a project when my phone rang. It was the attorney. He told me there was a little boy who was available for adoption. He was half-Caucasian, half-Hispanic. He asked three questions:

1. Is his ethnicity a problem for you? (*No.*)
2. Will you pay the medical bills for his birth? (*Yes.*)
3. Can you take him right away? (*Absolutely!*)

I left work and went home to tell my wife. As I walked in the door, she wondered why I was home at noon on a workday. I told her the attorney had called, and then I said, *"It's a boy!"*

As she began to cry, we embraced and celebrated the fact that Ericca would now be a big sister.

When you put a plan in place, you must be positive. Some friends had encouraged us through the process and recommended that we choose names for our next child, as a walk of faith.

That Friday afternoon, when we were in the attorney's office signing forms, the assistant said, "I know you don't have a name for him yet, so we will fill it in later." Proudly, we told her that we already had a name picked out. We named him after Shelley's dad, Jackson, and my brother, Jack. With a smile, she gladly wrote down the name Jackson James Hollister, born March 23, 1999.

For some legal reasons, we determined that we would pick him up from the hospital on Monday morning. As we entered the hospital area, we could see him in another room—a small bundle under a blue blanket. His black hair was sticking out of the top of the bundle.

We had not told anybody we were getting a baby, For a number of reasons. Yet we had spent the weekend getting ready. Fortunately, we still had a crib, and we set that up in the baby's room. Ericca was too young to understand what was going on. On this day, she was at preschool. I sat on the floor with the baby while my wife went to pick Ericca up from school.

You cannot imagine the joy we experienced upon watching this little girl walk into the family room. The baby was on a blanket on the floor. We explained that she had a new baby brother and that she was now a big sister, as she had wanted to be.

To confound the neighbors, I went to the local store and bought a large banner that said, "It's a Boy" and stapled it to the front of our garage. I also got matching Mylar balloons and tied them to the mailbox. It hadn't been nine months since we last saw our neighbors, and now there was a baby at the house.

Later that afternoon, we showed up at my brother's house with this huge surprise. My sister-in-law and her kids were thrilled with the new baby. Soon, my brother, Jack, got home and met his new namesake nephew. We called my mom and made some excuse about why she had to come into town. When she arrived, the three kids were sitting on the couch with a blanket across our laps and big grins on our faces.

With a flick of the wrist, we moved the blanket and revealed the newest grandchild to my mother. We have a picture of her at that moment with her mouth opened wide in complete amazement. It was a great day, and our family was finally complete.

Debt Stories

Our story about building our family through adoption is an example of a highly personal goal. For many people, their most important goal is to improve their financial situations.

Many of the personal-finance books I read in the early years were written by an author named Larry Burkett. He was a Christian author and radio host—the Dave Ramsey of his time. He did not have a following outside Christian circles as Dave does, but he was famous in the Christian realm nonetheless. He taught financial fundamentals to people. His books were easy to read, and many of his ideas were simple to implement. I am sure he did not create the "envelope system"; however, he taught it to people and explained the basics.

Back when people functioned with cash instead of plastic, the idea was that you created the categories of your budget and allotted a certain amount of cash each month for groceries, gas, utilities, auto repairs, clothing, etc. You put cash in the envelopes and then used the funds when you made a purchase. Mom would take the grocery envelope with her when she went to the market. She paid for her groceries with cash from the envelope and then put the receipt in the envelope, tracking her expenditures. She could see when the money was beginning to run out toward the end of the month, so she would cut back a little.

> You put cash in the envelopes and then used the funds when you made a purchase.

The money accumulated in the auto-repair envelope for weeks or months. And then, when our car needed a repair, my parents took the cash from the envelope and used it to pay for the repair.

It seems archaic now, but it is a great system. When someone is having a difficult time getting their arms around their expenses, the envelope system is a primary tool to help them get back on track. It enables you to *see* your money, which we don't really do anymore.

The steadily falling interest rates of the '90s created a false sense of well-being among those who would abuse their credit cards. My mortgage in 1989 was 10.5 percent. Though that seems high, people in the late '80s were paying more than 16 percent for their mortgages. It was not unusual for people to refinance their mortgage loans every three to five years. The smart people refinanced and kept the same payment, reducing their mortgage debt much more rapidly. Some had paid five years down on a thirty-year loan and went back up to thirty years to reduce their monthly payment. Many more refinanced, went back up to thirty years, and also rolled all their credit-card debt into the new loan.

They would reduce their credit-card debt to zero and lower their interest rate from 19.95 percent down to their mortgage rate. It gave people a false sense of freedom. Suddenly, they were out of debt (not including the mortgage); however, they hadn't fixed their propensity to overspend. Thus, they ran up their credit cards again and again, and then refinanced their mortgage in three to five years.

I know several people who did this many times. Each time, they moved back up to thirty years and rolled in their debt. Each time they refinanced, they usually added $4,000 to 5,000 in closing costs to the mortgage. The mortgage brokers said it was no big deal, and they would just roll it into the new loan. People didn't pay attention and continued to add credit-card debt and refinance costs on top of their mortgages. They were never getting ahead.

One guy I know has owned his home for twenty-eight years and still owes on his mortgage for twenty-three more years! Sounds ridiculous, but it's true. What people also did not realize was that their credit score continued to fall because of the ratio between their income and debt. Therefore, when they did get a credit card, the interest rates were often 15 percent and 19.95 percent. I even saw some at 24.95 percent. Try paying the minimum payment on a credit-card bill that is charging you 24.95 percent. You will be a little old person and still be making the payments—and I hope what you bought is still servicing you.

For most people who went down this path, the item was gone, yet the debt remained.

Eventually, these people hit a brick wall. They couldn't pay their credit card bills, and they couldn't refinance. Suddenly, years of bad habits came screaming into focus, with very few options. The credit-card companies are relentless, and the mortgage companies can repossess your home. It made for some very unpleasant situations and desperate times for many people.

Through a Sunday-evening education program at church, I began teaching a basic financial concepts class. It didn't take long before I was meeting people in the scenario above. To the best of my ability, I began to help them get out of debt. The Larry Burkett book had some outlines for reducing debt, and I used these concepts to help people. Back then, he called it "the debt ladder." Dave Ramsey refers to it as "the debt snowball," but the process is exactly the same.

Because this is a goals book, I will not dwell on the debt-ladder concept. Suffice it to say that if a person or a couple embraces the regimen, they can work their way out of debt. It takes more time than people would like, but it provides a winning strategy that gives people a sense of accomplishment and victory over time. Most people pay minimum payments on their cards and throw an extra $5 or $10 per month on to make them feel better. That doesn't get them very far toward reducing their debt.

Using the "Debt Ladder" Concept

The premise of the debt ladder is that you pay *all* extra money you receive toward the credit card with the smallest balance and make minimum payments on everything else. Once the first card is paid off, you take that monthly payment, plus the extra, and apply it to the card with the next-smallest balance. You continue to do this with each card paid. As you climb the ladder (or the snowball increases), your monthly payment on each progressive card gets larger, and you pay it off faster.

With this strategy, no consideration is made for interest rates. You make minimum payments on all cards except the one with the smallest balance. Each time you pay off a card, you close the account.

Accept Personal Responsibility for the Debt

The first thing I found with helping people reduce their debt was the agonizing process of them admitting that they had created the problem. Besides, they and only they were going to be responsible for getting themselves out. If only one person from a couple wants to get out of debt and the other does not, it will never work. A couple must work on reducing debt together, or one partner will undermine all the work the other partner does.

The other thing I realized was that I could not (I repeat, *could not*) get people out of debt. I could guide them and teach them the fundamentals. Yet I could not make the day-to-day decisions that are required for them to begin spending less and saving more.

> A couple must work on reducing debt together, or one partner will undermine all the work the other partner does.

In the early days of helping people, I tried to direct as much of their spending as possible; however, unless I traveled with them day and night, it was not possible for me to influence their spending. Most people know their monthly bills, but it is the cash expenditures and spur-of-the-moment purchases that get them into trouble.

One of the first things a person or a couple has to admit is that the system has outfoxed them. The banking and credit system has sold them a bill of goods, and it has trapped them. I tell people that the credit card and debt system is designed to get you hooked early and keep you in debt for your lifetime. At some point, you have to realize that the system is rigged. No one goes into a casino figuring that they have the upper hand on the house. But people go into debt all the time, not realizing that the deck is stacked against them.

Admitting that you have been foolish with your funds throughout your working life is a difficult thing to swallow. I have found that it is much more productive to focus on the future. If the debt has been making people's lives uncomfortable, such as receiving recurring collection calls, they are often ready to buckle down and get to work. They set a goal of getting their finances under control so they can ease the discomfort.

The first step they need to take is to agree to live below their means. This always will be the first primary rule of finance—*spend less than you make*. Often, though, when I tell people that, they look at me like I'm stupid. To stay out of debt, and to save for the future, of course you must spend less than your income. Yet everybody I know with personal debt spends much more than their income.

The second step is for them to agree not to add any more debt to the cards. This can be quite an adjustment. Many people carry only plastic and no cash. They are not accustomed to tracking their expenses or making sure there is money to cover each expense before the expense is incurred. Suddenly, the thought of going out for dinner on Saturday night becomes a major point of discussion because they must pay for it now, not months later on the credit-card bill.

These types of issues can cause a real change in people's lifestyle. That is why couples and families must agree to work together to adopt good habits and reach their target.

> "Chains of habit are too light to be felt until they are too heavy to be broken."
> —Warren Buffet

Goals Are Key to the Process

Setting realistic goals in this process is critical. It would be nice to throw an extra $500 against the credit card bills every month, but if the budget allows for only $150, then $150 it is. As soon as some funds get freed up, apply it to the debt. Again, all extra funds go to the card with the smallest balance. Once the first card is paid off, celebrate a little, and then begin working on paying off the next card.

Many times, I have witnessed how effective this process is. I've seen so many people who worked hard, trying to pay off their debt on several cards for years, yet never paying off any of them. Then suddenly, using this strategy, in a few months, they have paid off one card and are progressing toward the second.

It is the first time they feel like they have ever made any progress. Once they get this feeling, look out! They often catch the vision for what is happening and put every spare dime against their debt. Many people have postponed vacations and other purchases to hammer their debt down.

One lady came to me from the church. She had eight credit cards with a total balance of $32,000 and had been working with a credit consolidation company. In four years, she still had eight cards, with a total balance of $28,000. She had made little progress. I showed her how to use the debt-ladder strategy and in the next four years, using the debt ladder, she was entirely out of debt. On a couple of her smallest cards, she owed only a couple hundred dollars. With all the extra going toward the lowest debt, she paid off the first couple of cards quickly (and closed the accounts, I might add). She would catch me in church and tell me that she had paid off another card. She was so excited to be getting control of her life again.

The other thing that can happen is that people begin to look beyond the debt. For example, if you are paying $1,500 per month against credit cards, and you get out of debt in three years, then over the following three years, you can save $1,500 per month for yourself. That is $18,000 per year. At the end of another three years, you are not only out of debt but sitting on about $54,000 in cash. If you create the vision, set the goals, and take the appropriate actions, it is incredible what you can accomplish.

Here is a brief summary of the four steps you need to take to pay off your debt using the debt ladder:

1. Admit the problem.
2. Create a plan and goals.
3. Execute/take action.
4. Celebrate!

My Weight-Loss Story

I am not a licensed counselor and do not pretend to understand all the psychological issues that can be connected to many bad habits. With regard to debt, most people outside the family do not know there is a problem. With overweight people, however, it is apparent that there is an issue. Many people have been overweight for their entire lives.

Many times, there are deep issues that plague these people, and they may need the help of a professional counselor. If they were teased as children or ridiculed over the years, this would leave deep scars. They may suffer from poor self-esteem. For this section, I am going to deal with the habits and changes needed to lose weight, assuming there is no need for a counselor.

In my case, I believe I was destined to be big. My father was 6'2", 325 pounds. His mother's last name was Fuller. Her sister was 6 feet tall. They used to say, "Fuller people are big people." Because my grandfather was only 5'6", Dad must have gotten his size from the Fullers.

I was 6 feet tall by the ninth grade and settled in at 6'3" and about 220 pounds in my senior year in high school. I played tackle on the football team. My brother, Jack, was an inch shorter and about the same weight. Between my dad, my brother, and me, we made a wall. The expectation was that we were big people. By the time I was in junior high, the phrase had changed: "Hollister men are big men." Just a note: my mom was only 5'6".

As I grew older, I got heavier. I was not overweight as a child. Pictures of me in grade school showed a child of a slender or average build. I gained a good deal of weight in the ninth grade, after being sidelined from sports with appendicitis. Back then, you could do no athletics for at least six weeks after an appendectomy. I was never encouraged to watch my weight and was never discouraged from eating whatever I wanted.

After I began working, I lost considerable weight at times and keep it off for a while. However, I would eventually put it back on and deal with it again. My personal self-image was of a big man. When I lost weight, I felt slight and small. Big men are strong! Hollisters are big men!

I managed the ups and downs of my weight for many years. However, when I was sick in 1991, one of the medications they put me on was steroids. That added 40 pounds to my overweight frame, and I ballooned up to 285 pounds. I struggled with the weight for many years. It did not seem to hinder my business success, so it just became a way of life.

In 2014, I got the opportunity to speak at a breakout session at the Million Dollar Round Table (MDRT) meeting in New Orleans. My picture was going to be in the program, up on the screen, and about 1,400 people were going to see me. In the year before that, I determined that I was not going to be that fat-faced guy in a suit. I had a friend who had been successful in a weight-loss program, and I signed up for it. Over the course of the next six months, I dropped sixty-five pounds. When I

> Over the course of the next six months, I dropped sixty-five pounds.

spoke in New Orleans, I showed up in a new suit (old ones were too big) and weighed 230—the lowest I had been since high school.

There was something powerful about being seen in front of all those people that made me override all my excuses for not losing weight. I was more worried about being embarrassed than I was about potentially being unhealthy. There I was, setting out to teach these people something about goals. Were they going to listen to what I had to say or disregard me because of my weight? I wasn't taking any chances.

I chose to lose the weight. I sought out the program. I fixed healthy food, including salads, every day. I did not expect my wife to do it. I shopped for the items I needed; they were different from some of the groceries the family was using. My wife was very supportive (and very shocked) at first. She had poked and prodded me over the years to lose weight for health reasons. I hadn't listened, nor had I changed. Even when my dad died at the young age of sixty-three with heart issues, it really didn't make me change.

Because I had a distinct goal and a real deadline (June 2014), I was very determined to succeed. I embraced the program and never complained. This time, it was my idea, and I was going to lose the weight. Most heavy people have three wardrobes: fat pants, skinny pants, and in-between pants. I was so excited when I fit into a pair of my in-between pants. It had been years. They were out of style because it had been so long since I wore them. It didn't matter. Wearing an item of clothing that would have strangled me a few months earlier gave me a great sense of accomplishment.

Habits of Life

Setting goals to change bad habits relating to your personal life can be different from specific, one-time goals. If you have a goal to run a marathon, you train to work up to that goal, run the marathon, and then check it off your list. You may continue to run over the years or not, but you have completed the goal.

Life habits, such as losing weight, quitting smoking, stopping drinking, and managing anger, are different. You never quite accomplish those goals entirely. You are always revisiting the issue. Even when you think you finally have it whipped, something pops up to remind you that you still must manage it after all these years.

Once you go through the process of losing weight, you must then maintain it. You cannot drop fifty pounds on some weight-loss plan and then go back to eating ice cream out of the carton when you feel the urge. You must continue to make good choices. If you get off track, you must make decisions to get back on track. People yo-yo diet because they lose the weight and put it back on. Lose it and gain it back. Lose it and gain it back. There is an ongoing aspect of the goal. You never really achieve it; you learn to manage it in the new phase, with daily, healthy choices.

> You cannot drop fifty pounds on some weight-loss plan and then go back to eating ice cream out of the carton when you feel the urge.

The same goes for quitting smoking. I can remember guys in college trying to stop smoking. They would do fine from Sunday to Thursday. On Friday, with a beer in one hand, they seemed to need a cigarette in the other. The same may go for anger management. You do well for a while, then something sets you off, and you think, "Wow! I still have work to do."

Some habit-related goals can be made easier or more difficult, depending on your surroundings. If you come from a family of overweight people who have poor eating habits, then getting your cup of yogurt while everyone else eats fried chicken can be a difficult thing to do. To make matters worse, sometimes those family members tease you or ridicule you for trying to lose weight.

Deep down, they do not want you to succeed because that will make them look bad.

On the flip side, maybe you work with people who are physically fit and eat a balanced diet. It is part of their lifestyle, and they begin sharing ideas with you. Because the circle encourages fitness and good eating habits, it makes it easier for you to participate. In this scenario, I think you would be much more comfortable with your yogurt cup instead of a leftover piece of fried chicken. If *they* are going to the gym, then they understand why *you* go to the gym.

Trigger Points

The other thing you begin to realize when pursuing goals is what I refer to as "trigger points." You start to identify the elements in your life that trigger your bad habit. Maybe you manage your finances pretty well, but when you are stressed, you shop. Suddenly, you have credit-card debt and many items you don't need. Identifying *why* you do what you do will help you change the action in the future.

If you know that a particular relative seems to get your dander up, then you have three choices. You can avoid that person, let him or her set you off, or decide to measure your response. You take a couple of deep breaths, tell yourself you will not react. Maybe you keep your visit short, to prevent those trigger points from happening. You can't cut yourself off from the outside world, so you learn to manage triggering situations. I have individual relationships like this.

Maybe you have a friend whom you enjoy spending time with. You get along great, but you just happen to disagree on the political party in office. You both know those discussions end up in a quasi-argument. You are not going to change, and neither are they. I find it best just not to discuss that subject. There are usually plenty of common-ground subjects you can discuss without going down that road. If the issue comes up, or your friend makes a comment, you just say, "I think we need to agree to disagree."

It is more important to maintain the relationship than to bang that drum.

Going Back to College

We have discussed going back to college several times. I mention it again here because it is such an important and common priority for many people. This is a big goal that encompasses numerous subgoals, decisions, and actions.

This is not a single goal, but a series of goals and tasks that lead you to a permanent change in your education status and then an improvement in your work status and opportunities. Let's create a scenario.

Let's assume you are a mother or a father who works a full-time job and is responsible for two children. Your day is already full before you get out of bed on Monday morning, let alone adding the task of completing a college education. If you are going to school full-time, then you and your partner must have agreed on this by now. You have figured out that you can provide for the family on one income and incur the expenses of college going forward. You may decide to take out loans to pay for some of the education.

Your decision to get your education is predicated on one of the following situations. Either you have decided that your current training does not allow for opportunities in the workplace, or you are in a position where you have a bachelor's degree and need to pursue a master's or PhD to further your income opportunities. Either way, there should be an increase in income for you, the student, at the end of this process. The result will be an overall positive effect on the family finances.

A friend of mine with two kids quit his full-time job and got his master's in counseling and family psychology. His wife supported the family during those two years. As a result, he joined a counseling practice and has done very well for himself. This has had a profound impact on the family's income and overall well-being. They made a short-term sacrifice for long-term gain.

> They made a short-term sacrifice for long-term gain.

Just make sure that the education and degree you pursue have a positive financial impact that's worth the cost and sacrifice. Getting a degree that doesn't lead to real job opportunities is a waste of everybody's time and energy.

One thing that is interesting about these situations is the determination that I find in many students who return to college after being in the workforce for a while. First of all, they are not eighteen anymore. They are not going to join a fraternity/sorority, go uptown and party on the weekend, or engage in many other of the distractions that can arise with a student going to college right out of high school. There are also no room and board costs because the student is commuting or taking classes online.

Once you know your school schedule, you and your partner will decide who will take the kids to school or daycare, when you will study (without interruption), and many other decisions involved in running the household. Maybe your partner has to adjust his or her work schedule to be more available to the kids so you can excel in your classes. Without going into every detail, you will both need to adjust your lives so you can complete your education. This could be for two or more years. If going part-time, it could take several years.

So at the top of your goal sheet, you will write "Get My Degree in Family Counseling" or "Get My MBA" or "Get my degree in education so I can teach." It is only one line on the paper, but it is going to lead to hundreds of lines of activity to accomplish. Let's see if I can help you break it down with the reverse pyramid.

Goal:

Obtain my MBA (Master of Business Administration)

Subgoals and Actions Needed:

1. Decide which school to attend.
2. Determine how much time it will take.
3. Calculate how much will it cost—tuition, books, computer, etc.
4. Decide with your partner how to handle day care if you still have young kids. Can the grandparents or other relatives help?
5. Estimate how many hours per week are required for class time and study time.
6. Calculate the approximate income benefit the new degree will allow you to provide for your family.
7. Describe the other impacts the process will have on your family And on your spouse's work schedule.
8. If an internship will be involved, determine how will you and your spouse work around that schedule, if it's different from class hours. If you want to pursue an education degree, plan with your spouse how you will work around your student-teaching schedule when the time comes.
9. Determine the financial impact of this goal on the family. Will the family need to change some of its spending habits to reach the goal? Maybe there won't be any vacations for the next couple of years, or you and your spouse choose

not to buy Christmas and birthday gifts for each other for a time.

10. Establish the time frame for the goal:

Year 1:

- Semester 1—Classes A, B, C, and D
- Semester 2—Classes E, F, G, H
- Summer Session—Classes I, J

Year 2:

- Semester 1—Classes K, L, M, N
- Semester2—Classes O, P, Q, R
- Internship
- Graduation

Do I hear a celebration?

This timeline depends on getting a passing grade in some courses before you will be able to take courses that follow them. Therefore, poor performance in any class may delay the process. Also, papers and/or projects will be required in some classes. You will need to perform them satisfactorily and on time to earn a good grade in each class. The assumption is that you are going to complete all assignments in the process of achieving the goal.

I think you get the picture. It is easy to sit down and write a goal on a piece of paper. It isn't too difficult to delineate it and outline the general process to get there. However, it is an entirely different thing to walk out the specific details and the timeline. This is why goal setting can be so overwhelming at times.

It's also why it can be beneficial to get a friend or mentor to walk with you through this process. I guarantee you will get frustrated and want to quit. It can be helpful to have somebody by your side to help you focus on the end result and the long-term benefit that will come from this sacrifice.

You Manage What You Measure

When setting goals, there is typically something to measure. With weight loss, it is calories or carbs. With weight lifting, it is weights and reps. With sales goals, it is amount of revenue and number of presentations. Unless you have something to measure, how do you know how you are doing?

I am not a runner, but many friends who run tell me they either measure their time or have certain milestones along their route that help them know their progress. Imagine heading out for a marathon run and having no mile markers and no watch to tell the time. I would think it would be difficult to pace yourself, and you would have little idea of where you are in the process.

> Unless you have something to measure, how do you know how you are doing?

Personal Accountability

Years ago, when I was young and thought I knew everything, my sales manager came up with a program that he titled "Personal Accountability." I thought it was the dumbest thing I had ever heard. He kept going on about how this had such a dramatic impact on salespeople who had embraced it. I was doing fine, hitting my goals, and I didn't need such a ridiculous notion—police—to oversee my day.

Boy, was I wrong!

Once I got past the rhetoric and started to listen, I realized that the only way we ever improve is if we take on a role and are accountable to ourselves first. I have watched salespeople try to meet the company's requirements, their sales manager's (my) requirements, or their spouse's requirements. At the end of the day, those requirements were nothing more than a quota written on a sheet of paper. There was no ownership by the salesperson and no buy-in. There was no drive to push through the difficult days.

However, I noticed a big difference in people who had a real need to succeed. They had something in them that was pushing them. This drive got them up in the morning, and that helped them make one or two more sales calls at the end of the day. I have always thought it was desire and pure survival instinct. What I soon came to understand was that it was personal accountability.

Psychology probably has many names for it. You could call it hutzpah, drive, or inner desire. I used to call it "the jazz"—that feeling that comes over you when everything is lining up and going your way. In personal sales, this sense of well-being and self-confidence can have a dramatic impact on results over time.

Even if you are not in sales, I want to give you a perspective of the mental battle that can go on each day for those who are. I am sure it is similar, regardless of your line of work.

If you recall, my sales job was working in small towns or plaza areas of cities, calling directly on small retailers. We sold custom labels, tags, pricing guns, and imprinted bags. It is not a scenario that you would see much today, but in the 1980s and early '90s, it was a very viable model. Now we have superstores like Walmart, as well as online ordering.

Back then, every small town had clothing stores, record stores, office-supply shops, pet shops, and usually Christian bookstores. The owners were the salt of the Earth, and they made a good living owning and managing their stores. Because the areas were more compact, the owners had good relationships in the community and with their clientele.

That was before we had cell phones. We called into the office each day on an 800 number to check with our customer-service person and to follow up on orders. I knew all the convenient places to get a cup of coffee, use the restroom, and use a pay phone to make some calls. You seldom see pay phones any longer. I often think how much more territory I could have covered if we had cell phones back then.

Assuming a salesperson got trained and had what it took to do the job, there were always distractions to keep you out of the field. The first issue was always the weather. It could be hot, cold, rainy, snowy, or all the above. The home office was states away, and we were responsible for getting into our sales territory on our own. It was easy to get distracted at home and get out late. It was also easy for a friend to ask for help or favors and leave the territory early. Unfortunately, it was easy to stay home if you weren't "feeling it."

There was always paperwork to do, service phone calls to make, and problems to solve. If you were not really in "the mood" to make sales calls, it was amazing what you could find to distract yourself.

However, the successful reps had an entirely different MO. They got up early and made sure they were into their territory as soon as retailers were open. They made sales calls all morning and took a brief lunch break sometime after one o'clock. Many store owners were in their stores through the lunch hour, so going to lunch at noon for the rep meant missing perfect opportunities.

These reps made calls up and down the street and in the plazas. When they got the opportunity to meet with a client, they didn't demonstrate just one idea or product, but three or four. It was a very pleasant presentation, and the products met the needs of the small retailers, who were trying to compete against the bigger chain stores. It was common to call on twenty to twenty-five businesses per day.

After lunch and a call to the office, then the successful reps were back to making sales calls. If the owner was busy or not in, you moved down the street and circled back to talk to them. My best town was Titusville, Pennsylvania. It was about sixty miles north of Pittsburgh and forty miles south of Erie, on the western side of the state. It was twenty minutes to the next four-lane highway, and it thrived. Over a ten-year period, I served forty of the forty-four retail businesses in the area.

Over a period of ten years, I had more than one thousand businesses that had become customers in my sales territory. Many of them bought multiple products from me. The business owners came to see me as a key supplier for them in their desire to market and promote their businesses.

Personal accountability came into play as a way to manage our goals and keep our minds on the big goal, while pursuing the goals of the day. The challenge came in working a complete day. If you made goals for all your activity, such as how many calls you would make, how many sales you would make, and how much you would earn in commissions, then you also needed goals for what you wanted to earn each week, month, and year.

Here is a typical planning scenario; I would write down daily goals to plan my income for a week:

- Write three pieces of business—average order $250.
- Make $150 per day—based on a commission of 20 percent on key items for five days—$750 for the week.
- 50 Weeks, $37,500—a pretty good income in the late '80s

These were reasonable goals for an experienced rep in an existing territory. The key word here is *goals*, plural—hitting just one goal was not sufficient. I had to reach all my goals.

Maybe I wrote three orders by the time I had made four calls. Did I quit because I'd already met my quota? No. Why? Because I also had a goal of making twenty calls for the day. The fact that I hit my order goal didn't overshadow the fact that my call goal was twenty businesses.

If I wrote one large order and made $200 from that order, did I quit for the day? No. I still had not written three pieces of business, nor had I called on twenty business owners. If I made a sale on the first item I showed the owner, did I pack my kit and walk? No. I was not greedy, but I did want to make sure the owner knew what else I had. Besides, my goal was to show three to four products per sales call. If I made my quota of $750 by Thursday, did I still work on Friday? Of course—because that was my commitment to myself.

If a manager was standing over me, watching my every move, I am sure I would have had some descriptive words for him or her. The manager's expectations would undoubtedly seem unreasonable.

Or would they?

Personal accountability comes into play in managing the mind games we play with ourselves. It keeps us going down the road and focusing on the long-term picture. You do not need a manager standing over you, telling you to keep going. You do that for yourself. I will speak for myself when I say I am much more apt to do what I think is right than to need someone else to tell me to do it. Even if what they told me is right, I would resent the fact that they told me. Stubborn, I know.

Personal accountability is the ability to stand in the mirror and have an honest conversation with yourself. Because nobody else is in the room, you can use any descriptive language you like. Call yourself names, or tell

Personal accountability is the ability to stand in the mirror and have an honest conversation with yourself.

yourself you are the most fantastic salesperson, spouse, employee, parent in the world. And then do everything in your power to make it happen. No excuses. No distractions.

Our most successful salespeople got up early, got into their territories early, made necessary phone calls, and kept the phone time to a minimum. They serviced their existing clients in person and made cold calls for new opportunities. They stayed in their territories until the retail stores closed. If the weather was bad, they looked at their schedule and picked a town that was closer, saving the distance travel for a clearer day.

How does personal accountability impact the goal-setting process and all that we have talked about throughout this book? At the end of the day, it is you against the world. If you are a believer, it is you and God against the world, but you are still the one who must go to work, get up early, and stay late. You are the one who must control your eating, drinking, cursing, anger, or any other harmful habit you are trying to change.

You Are in Charge of Your Future

If you had seen my bathroom wall back in the early goal-setting days, you would have thought I was crazy. I had quotes taped to the mirror and walls from the greats like Zig Ziglar, Brian Tracy, and Jim Rohn. I had quotes from *Think and Grow Rich* and *The Art of Thinking Big*. I also had Scriptures; words of encouragement; and pictures of houses, boats, and cars I liked. I was determined to get my workday off to a great start, and seeing these visual reminders helped me keep my mind on track.

However you choose to embrace personal accountability, it must become a way of life for you. You must decide you are in charge of your future, your income, and your destiny. This is especially true when you are pursuing long-term goals. It sounds dramatic, but it is true. Nobody cares more about you than you do, and hopefully, your spouse.

If you are trying to lose weight, then do the shopping for yourself. Do not make excuses that the proper food is not in the fridge. Make your salad yourself in the morning, and make sure you drink enough water. Count your calories on absolutely everything you eat, and don't cheat. If you do, you are only cheating yourself.

If you are trying to manage your anger, then the first thing you must do is realize you need to change. The second thing you must do is apologize to those you have hurt. Talk to your family members, and ask them for help, prayer, and patience. Then be kind when they remind you that you just hurt their feelings. It can be a team effort, but you are ultimately responsible.

If you want to grow at work, then sit down with your boss or mentor and ask them to tell you what they see and how they think you can improve. After you lick your wounds, embrace the journey and then begin working on those areas. Maybe you need a book or a class, or perhaps you just need to learn to listen and work as a team. All these skills can be learned.

Personal accountability must become a way of life for you— not a religion, but a lifestyle that propagates the life you want. It is much more than just setting goals. It is the only way to overcome all the disciplines you choose and to be accountable *to* yourself, and *for* yourself. You must be responsible to yourself to set your day in order.

I believe that if you make this transition, you will see the fruit of the disciplined life that you need and sincerely want. You must include all areas of your life in personal accountability: work, play, sleep, prayer, love, church, children, spouse, and friends. At the end of the day, you will have a real measure of what you have accomplished and what needs to change in your future.

You are the best there is. People like you are the people who change the world. Start with changing and making yourself better. Help those around you improve. Then, hopefully, you will get the chance to change the world in some fashion. Sponsor a child, start a business, go on a mission trip. You can accomplish almost everything if you put your mind and energy into it. And along the way, don't forget to love those around you.

"And now abide faith, hope, love, these three; but the greatest of these is love."
—1 Corinthians 13:13

Can you look in the mirror every night before you go to bed and say to yourself, "I have done my best today"? If the answer is yes, then give yourself credit.

Congratulations on your future success! I wish you all the best as you set out on your journey toward *getting there.*

ABOUT THE AUTHOR

For most of Carleton "Holly" Hollister's career, he has been in sales of some kind. With a solid understanding of numbers, he always made sales goals a focus in his business plan. As he learned that process, he quickly began to understand other aspects of goal setting to help him achieve goals in other important areas of life.

As Holly grew in his sales career, he began to apply the goal-setting process to each aspect of life: how to be a better spouse and father, how to get out of debt and begin to save and invest. Along the way, he was fortunate enough to have many mentors who were willing to coach him.

In his early years at Century Marketing, he was introduced to the great motivators of the time—Brian Tracy, Dale Carnegie, Napoleon Hill, and Jim Rohn. He even spent time at a Zig Ziglar training class and met Zig in person. This training and the books and tapes that came with it have been a foundation of learning for Holly's career and growth. From salesperson to sales trainer to sales manager and then national recruitment manager for his company, he mentored those around him, as others had mentored him.

In 2001, Holly started his own company, Hollister Financial, as a wealth-management professional and financial advisor. Taking the training he had gotten as he worked through his own financial goals, and with his experience helping others get out of debt, Holly began helping individuals learn to save and plan for their financial future. Partnering with Savage and Associates, from Toledo, Ohio, he continued his education and growth with exposure to sales leaders, including John Savage and Million Dollar Round Table (MDRT) leaders.

He is a member of several prestigious organizations, including MDRT, and accomplished the highest level of qualification. He is a member of the Academy of Preferred Financial Advisors (APFA), an organization that trains the best financial advisors to be better. He is also a member of NAIFA, an organization that represents insurance and financial advisors and provides them with additional training so they can stay abreast of industry and political changes in our business.

Holly continues to grow his practice and strives to serve as many clients as possible. His State Retirement Roadshow seminars are well-attended and continue to educate teachers and state employees on their State of Ohio retirement options. Backing him up is a team of dedicated professionals, working hard each day to assist clients as they reach for their goals. We never stop learning!

"The investment environment is always changing. We are here to help people understand their options."
—Carleton "Holly" Hollister

---

www.ingramcontent.com/pod-product-compliance
Lightning Source LLC
Chambersburg PA
CBHW060910120626
46553CB00001B/272